NEW EARTH
BRINGING IT HOME

A LIGHT HEARTED

TRANSFORMATIONAL JOURNEY

Joy-An Tucker

Joy Rising Publications

Mt. Shasta

Copyright © 2022 Joy-An Tucker

All rights reserved.

No part of this book may be used or reproduced in any way without permission from the author except for short quotes with credit given to the author.

IngramSpark Printing

ISBN: 978-09622061-2-2

ABOUT THE AUTHOR

Although I am a former college teacher with three master degrees and have been a student of ascended masters for over 20 years and several spiritual pathways, what really matters is that I am a wayshower who applies wisdom and knowledge in my daily life and learn and teach from direct experience as I do in my books and life coaching. It is my joy and my passion to offer healing with horses on my ranch near Mt. Shasta California and to live my vision of New Earth. It is my passion and my purpose to share the vision and experience of New Earth qualities as I inspire others to experience greater joy, happiness, love, and peace in their own lives through consciousness coaching, Creator connection attunements, and spiritual home decorating consultations.

New Earth: Bringing It Home, Joy-An Tucker's new book, is fun to read and simple to grasp. It's filled with down-home (literally!) experiences, humor and wisdom, and includes helpful practices any of us can do. I highly recommend it to anyone who enjoys clearing out the old to create a lighter, spiritually based, happier life. – *Joanna Cherry, author* of *Living Mastery*

Joy-An is a pioneer. This book is far more than a do it yourself decorating guide. Blending practical application with the universal vibrations of spirit, her compelling journey has shown me a new way of "seeing" my home. She has refreshed my deeper vision. *Victoria Hall, retired interior decorator*

Despite the heady concepts, Tucker's guidance is refreshingly clear, laying out the steps for a journey of introspection and vision-realization in prose that will appeal both to seasoned spiritual searchers and readers new to recognizing "the power of Creator's light within you." Tucker's warm tone and personal anecdotes, encouraging explanations of topics like "intention" and sacred geometry, and her linking of the spiritual to home decor "that which makes your heart sing" all result in a calming, engaging read that persuasively conveys a larger message of love, unity, and balance. – *BookLife/Publishers Weekly*.

What makes this guide stand out from the pack is its emphasis on practical steps (breathing exercises and meditation prompts, bringing nature indoors, balancing colors, making one's bathroom beautiful) that, before ascension, will certainly increase one's peace of mind. -*BookLife/Publishers Weekly*

DEDICATION

I dedicate this book to all those who are awakening to their greater selves or who are about to awaken in their own best timing

Contents

DEDICATION v

ACKNOWLEDGMENTS ix

INTRODUCTION: IT ALL STARTS WITH YOU xi

PART 1, INTERTWINING INNER AND OUTER 1

Bedbugs! 3

Unicorns and Blue Rays 7

The Inner Temple 15

Letting Go: Easier Said Than Done? 21

Golden Treasures 25

Green Grass and a Stroke of Luck 33

Purple Mountain Majesty 39

Pink Pyramid 45

Sliding into White 49

Bathroom Break 53

PART 2, SACRED GEOMETRY, SOUND, SPACE 57

Circles, Curves, and Lightships 59

Mandelbrot, Anyone? 63

The Sound of hOMe 67

A Space of Love 73

PART 3, UNITY IN RELATIONSHIP 75

Cease arguing! Harmony in Relationship 77

Your Joy is Your Passion 81

Reverence for All Life 85

Oneness with All Life 89

Kind Eyes	91
Freedom	93
Freedom of the Unknown	97
Dolphins and Rainbows	99
Connecting with Creator	103
AFTERWORD	107
ADDITIONAL READING AND LISTENING	109

ACKNOWLEDGMENTS

Thank you to all my teachers: ascended masters, angels, people, horses, dogs, cats, and my own I AM

Thanks especially to Ashamarae333@gmail.com for amazing private sessions with St. Germain

Thank you Victoria Hall for your suggestions and your review.

Thank you Hay House Writers' Community for great guidance.

Thank you xee_designs1 at Fiverr.com for patient professional formatting and cover design.

INTRODUCTION: IT ALL STARTS WITH YOU

I have a dream to inspire people throughout the world to hold the vision until it becomes our reality. It starts with you, with all of us: bringing New Earth home.

For me it all started with bedbugs. I'll come back to that. Let me update you first.

- It is time. It's time for miracles. Time for old patterns and paradigms to fall away in everyone, in you, in the whole world—to be replaced by something much better, much lighter
- It's time to step up, to raise your vibration even more, to live from your heart in communion with Creator, expressing Creator's love, harmony peace, joy in every part of your life, inner and outer. No buts
- It's time to acknowledge your truth—that you are a child, an expression, a fractal of Creator, a divine, radiant sun in your own right.
- It's time to recognize the power of Creator's light within you and within the world.
- It's time to live your passion, live your joy.
- It's time to be a conscious expression of Source, the One, in every moment.
- It's time for manifestation of that which you envision and wish to create.

Right now you can create an oasis of love and harmony in the very midst of change and chaos, in the midst of disharmony all around, until the Divine

Plan for New Earth is fully realized, when all humanity knows oneness, unity, and reverence for all life. It all starts with you as you make yourself and your home a temple of New Earth, or if you prefer, a sacred space of love. Intent matters, not labels.

The good news is that the trail has been blazed. A critical mass has been reached of awakened humans who are consciously radiating light and love on this planet. The evolutionary process of moving from the third dimension to the fifth and beyond is therefore speeding up and a bit easier than ever before.

If you want to be one in that number, set your intention by saying out loud:

Beloved Creator, who I AM also. I now harmonize with the Divine plan to ascend humanity, planet Earth, and all beings upon her.

You have been heard. So it is.

WHAT IS NEW EARTH? If you are new to this kind of perspective, you may not yet know that Gaia or Mother Earth is a conscious being. She has been raising vibration for a long time, meaning her atoms and electrons are vibrating faster and faster. (All matter consists of vibratory energy, like radio waves, even when it is solid.) Humans are also on the same trajectory, some consciously, some not. Mother Earth (Gaia) wants to take her children with her into higher frequencies, higher dimensions. That is ascension.

New Earth actually already exists—a higher dimensional, enlightened planetary being surrounding, infusing, enveloping the unascended form. Our own higher self does the same with each of us. As old friends used to say: FAR OUT!

As each of us awakens more and more to love, harmony, joy and oneness with all creation, these higher frequencies affect every cell, atom, electron, DNA. The stranglehold of a more limited reality relaxes and drops away. I, you, everyone is preparing to live on New Earth. Creating harmony in your home and relationships can be part of your spiritual path. Home decoration becomes a sacred mirror for your journey. You are a divine co-creator of New Earth through your intention alone.

PART 1

INTERTWINING INNER AND OUTER

1

BEDBUGS!

Bedbugs were the ruthless kick-in-the-butt that started me on my rededication and redecoration journey.

A few years before, during meditation, I had received inner guidance that the New Earth was only a step away in a parallel reality. With child-like trust I took that step, and felt myself bathed in the bliss of her frequencies. Inspired, I began envisioning my home as a Temple of New Earth, a destination, example, and teaching center on my horse ranch near Mt Shasta, California, a town that many spiritual seekers and vacationers visit because of the magnificent mountain that reigns over all.

As so often happens with such lofty plans and intentions, ordinary life and self-doubt got in the way because I allowed it. How could an 1800 square foot manufactured home surrounded by horse corrals, a barn, and pastures and full of shabby furniture be a temple? I did not have the courage and self-trust or the funds to move forward with my vision. I also had just begun a healing with horses program at my ranch, Joy Rising Ranch, so visitors were coming to experience the magic of my gifted horses. Covid rules and regulations also interfered with plans.

One of the ways I generated income for myself was through short-term rentals of one of my bedrooms to Mt Shasta tourists. This area has a history of Ascended Master St. Germain appearing and teaching on Mount Shasta in the 1930's. You can feel the high vibration of the area as soon as you arrive and feel its absence when you leave. Many people come also to connect with Telos, a fifth dimensional city of light said to be located under the mountain and the whole area. According to the lore, this city was founded by Lemurians who took refuge here at the time of the fall of Atlantis.

Apparently, the latest guest had left a bedbug or two behind.

It started with lines of maddening itchy welts. I had experienced hay mites in the past, which stay a few days but cannot thrive on a human body. This new condition, however, kept getting worse, an indisputable itchy plague of some kind. Finally my long-term housemate, who rented my master bedroom, suggested it might be bedbugs, so I knelt by my bed to check the mattress. I noticed some dark dust nestled next to the piping, but nothing I could clearly declare as bedbugs, which I had never before experienced. A few hours later, my knees were covered with itchy welts. I let go of my denial.

My experienced housemate explained there was probably a nest somewhere in the bedroom. My intuition guided me to a box underneath my altar that contained all my identity documents—passport, birth certificate, deed to the house, teaching credentials and such. Opening it, I was shocked to see the black smudges and appleseed-like bugs that I had seen pictured on the internet. Oh boy! Now what?

I did not fail to register that symbols of my identity were being pooped on by these pests. Hmm. I'd think about that later. I quickly transferred the important contents of the box into a clear plastic container, took the original box to the trashcan, and the plastic box to the yard until I could figure out my next step. The unavoidable result was more lines of bites. I was acting coolly and methodically, but inside I was freaking the heck out.

I trucked my incredibly comfortable old queen bed and the twin guestroom bed to the dump and began sleeping on a trifold mattress on my living room floor while I treated my bedroom with hardware store remedies. About a week later, the infernal little bloodsuckers found me. My renter gave me thirty days notice and spent the nights elsewhere. Additional evidence had appeared in her bedroom. They spread fast.

I tried to communicate with the bugs and also called in higher frequencies to make the environment undesirable for them, but I had not yet mastered those alchemies. Finally I gave in to the expense of a professional pest control agent, who made an appointment a whole month away.

Meanwhile I sprayed peppermint essential oil mixed with grape seed oil around my floor mattress each night and slathered my legs and arms with Vicks Vaporub or essential oil sprays to discourage attacks. Nevertheless, my body became covered with more itchy welts. I lay awake each night dreading their approach, but they seemed to arrive only after I finally fell asleep each night, leaving more lines of bites.

I asked myself, "How and why did I create this" for I take full responsibility for all manifestations in my life. I refuse to be a victim.

I began throwing out almost all my furniture, mostly old yard sale stuff and furniture left behind by the previous owner: another bed, chairs, dresser, sofa, and more. I kept only the dining table, one upholstered chair, one nightstand, and the queen bed in the master bedroom, which my renter was about to vacate.

A bit obsessed, I also washed and dried, washed and dried several times over all clothes and bedding, throwing a lot of that out too in the process. I was on a ruthless roll—not what can I keep, but what can I discard.

The strange thing is, I really enjoyed throwing it all out, taking it to the dump. Like many people I usually cling to old things, avoid spending money, and try to keep the status quo; but the necessity for change was indisputable. I felt so much joy, even ecstasy, at emptying my house of everything that did not serve the vision of harmony and beauty I now craved to create, in spite of my limited income.

The same applied to my inner world of habitual patterns, social conditioning, negative thinking, and even cellular memory. It was time to release that which no longer served my ascension intentions, period, end of story. It was time to let go of all stories. I realized I had invited this aggressive invasion of bloodthirsty beasts. They were the perfect reflection of my constant thoughts of irritation with someone. My irritation and judgments had gained momentum, constantly running through my mind night and day like a hamster on an exercise wheel—or bedbugs.

Not only did I need to clean up my home; I needed to clean up my mind and the thought forms I was spewing into the environment. Simultaneously, I learned later that near the end of 2021 all of humanity was going through a purging process whether aware of it or not. More cosmic light was pouring into the planet than ever before to accelerate the ascension of all, sweeping debris in front of it like a tidal wave. So I was at a choice point—step up to the plate and collaborate with the Divine Plan and the new trajectory or succumb to low vibratory thinking, feeling, chaos and separation in my inner and outer world. I took the wave full on and rode it.

Using all my will and power, I withdrew attention from the persons who were the object of my irritation and instead held them in my heart with love. I added to my moments of sitting meditation—in which I labeled all thoughts as just thinking—walking, car driving, corral cleaning, and washing dishes meditations, as well, until the hamster wheel's death grip on my mind began to fade. I focused on my breathing. I renewed my vigilance for any unhelpful feelings and thoughts so I could cancel them before they became a creation in my reality. I wasn't perfect in this effort, but it made a difference. I also asked for all the help I could get from the angels, guides, ascended masters and galactic families of light on my ascension team. (We all have such a team once we decide to reach for the stars).

All of humanity is going through this cleansing and upshifting process. I expect you are too.

Summary of shifting tools in this chapter:

- Let your tyrants be your teachers
- Be willing to change.
- Free yourself from your tyrant teacher when the lesson has been learned.
- Use your will, power, and intent to align with Creator and the Divine Plan.
- Take the practical steps needed to change your inner and outer environment.
- Stop projecting your stuff onto someone else and take full responsibility.
- Throughout your daily activities label thoughts as just thinking rather than get sucked into your stories, and focus on your breathing.
- Ask for the help you need from all levels of creation serving the light.

2

UNICORNS AND BLUE RAYS

When I was a child, my world was a crayon box full of every color and hue. Colors were light, brilliant light, glowing light, some bright, some gentle and soothing. I liked blue. Blue for me was trust, peace. Blue blanket, blue shirt, dark blue night lit by the moon, light blue day lit by the sun, raying into infinity. I stepped into radiant blue. I was transparent, not solid. It filled my fingers, my toes, my nose, all of me, my heart.—Joy-An Tucker, *When I Was a Child: As Given By the Cosmic Christ*

After the demise of the bedbugs, my front living room was empty of chairs, sofa, and decoration. One of the first things I wanted to replace was the ancient green, yellow, and brown plaid sofa left behind by the previous owners eight years ago. It was already laid to rest at the dump. I imagined the peace and tranquility of blue in that room, no more red accents and Mexican blankets.

The blue ray that originated from Creator eons and eons ago, contains the qualities of divine will, power, joy, and trust. That is DIVINE will, not of the ego, and the power of Divine unconditional love. The blue ray is most commonly associated with Ascended Master El Morya and Archangel Michael. Mother Mary, Yeshua, and Krishna were indigo blue ray persons, meaning they came into embodiment carrying the qualities of this ray: the will and power to carry out Creator's intention, pure joy of life, and open-hearted faith and trust in Creator's plan. I too came in on the blue ray and am deeply connected to a blue sun in the Pleiadian star system. So this was to be my blue ray room.

I searched online stores for a blue sofa for a few days but found nothing suitable in my price range. During that time I saw a garage sale announcement that had a bed for sale, which I also needed. Although I did not want more second hand furniture, I was acquainted with the seller; so I called him to ask if I could come by a few days before the sale. While there I asked if by any chance he had a blue sofa for sale, thinking it was not likely but why not ask. He did! A beautiful blue velvet sofa in perfect condition for sixty dollars! After making sure he was not selling stuff because of bed bugs, I bought the couch and the full-size bed.

I was in the flow of manifestation, I realized, when such little miracles occur. A few days later as I ambled through Walmart, I saw the image of a radiant white unicorn shaded with lavender rearing on a snowy mountain ledge against a sapphire blue sky. The item inside the package was a plush throw. I tossed it in my shopping cart without a second thought, thrilled to have found this stunning art to hang above my new sofa. I hung it up as soon as I got home. It's effect was dramatic and awesome, the unicorn vibrant with dynamic strength, beauty, and energy.

Unicorns had come into my life just a few months before, again in Walmart. As I walked down the bedding aisle, I saw a cute plush unicorn with kind eyes and a pink mane and tail. Against all reason I knew I had to have it. Hugging it to my chest, I paid for it at the checkout counter, filled with joy and laughter as I left the store, my inner child very happy.

Sometimes I worked with Ascended Master St. Germain through an excellent channel. St. Germain, named after a town in France where he had lived in a previous century, had in an earlier lifetime been Joseph the father of Yeshua (Jesus is the Greek translation). An ascended master is one who has graduated from the Earth plane and is no longer subject to the cycles of birth and death. During my next session with Master St. Germain, I asked why I had been so drawn to a plush toy. He told me the unicorn realm was connecting to me, and I had responded without thought straight from my heart. The unicorns, he said, are the ascended masters of the animal kingdom, and they live in the seventh dimensional angelic realms. Their "horns" are spirals of light from their third eye that they use as a healing tool. They are master healers.

Moreover, one of the unicorns, a beautiful, elegant female elder, wanted to merge with my not-so-elegant healing horse Doc Happy. With Happy's and my permission, St. Germain facilitated the merging and said she would be one with Happy in his body until the mountain (Mt Shasta) opened up. I knew intuitively that such an opening would happen only when it was time for Telosians and other multidimensional beings to disclose themselves to a ready humanity, ready for New Earth and oneness with all life. This all might sound a bit far out to you, but in the town of Mt Shasta such perspectives are the norm.

The awesome unicorn gracing my wall above my blue couch was an expression of a new level of awareness in my life, a messenger of deep love, healing, oneness, and pure joy of life. I placed a couple of temporary blue camp chairs in the other end of the room opposite the couch so I could meditate and enjoy the view.

I was still in the flow of joyful manifestation, feeling as if all creation was tuning in and supporting my intention. A couple of weeks later, I attended a gathering at SHE of a Thousand Angels Temple in Mt Shasta (dedicated to Mary Magdalene). In the Angel Room there was a beautiful Turkish or Persian style polyester rug. I knew immediately that such a rug in blue would be the perfect enhancement to my blue ray room, which had a wall-to-wall sage green carpet.

A search online at Wayfair found it. I knew the minute I saw it that it was the one, no question. Made of polypropylene, it was affordable. I was excited as a child at Christmas when it was delivered to my door. I tore open the box and unrolled the carpet. It was perfect, a blue and ivory stunning Turkish print. But, oh my, it stank! Polypropylene gases off big time, I learned. I had to drape it over a porch rail outside for a whole month before I dared to bring it in.

It was worth it though for the beauty and the price, so attractive and complementary in my blue ray room. In the decorative center shined a blue and ivory symmetrical cross, which in many cultures and traditions represents the merging of spirit and matter. The merging of spirit and matter is a big step on every true spiritual path. It is part of the ascension process, the embodiment of higher vibratory aspects of ourselves consciously expressing Creator in human form in every moment, using divine power and will to manifest every other divine attribute—Divine love, harmony. unity, compassion, joy, wisdom, oneness with all life, and more.

Yes, the rug belonged in my Temple of New Earth, which it dawned on me I was finally creating both inwardly and outwardly.

The room already contained a predominately blue and ivory picture of White Buffalo Woman, painted by a Vedanta priest friend, rising out of a buffalo skull with a medicine pipe in her hands. Legend has it that she brought the pipe to the Lakota people and other Native American tribes to teach them to talk directly to Great Spirit. We can all do that even without the pipe. The tool served as a bridge.

Under the picture of White Buffalo Woman, I replaced one of the camp chairs with a real chair and ottoman that I found at a friend's moving sale. It was super comfortable, swiveled, and leaned back. However, taupe was not quite the right color. Dissatisfied, I wondered if I should move it into a bedroom. Then I remembered a blue silk shawl I had purchased a few years ago at a short-lived store in Mt Shasta. It was painted with a gold hawk on each end and feathers floating in the middle

Back when I was still living in Santa Barbara, California, during one week hawks in the area seemed to be trying to get my attention. One swept to the ground a short distance away. Another time as I was riding my mare Isharra (a beloved partner for thirty-six years), it swooped out of a tree in front of us, startling us both. The hawk later circled over my head and settled on a tree branch right next to the horse corral. When animals become that insistent, they should not be ignored; so I spoke.

"Hawk," I said. "What is your message, flying low through the trees, startling me and my horse with your beauty, red tails, broad wings, masters of air over grass?"

I made a song of their reply, and I did fly with them; but that is another story. The song began "It is time to fly, spread your wings and fly." A few verses later it ended with

Sky Dancer, do not fear to fly;

You do not leave Earth behind.

Air strokes Earth, whispers into her,

Into the trees, and all around you.

There is no separation, only joining.

Fly with me now, fly with me now.

Fly with me, fly with me.

Their song encouraged me then to enter a new dimension of perception and experience—that of flight or ascension on the inner planes while remaining physically present on earth. They spoke of a balance and interpenetration between heaven and earth, spirit and body.

I placed the silk hawk shawl lengthwise on the chair, and that made all the difference. Now the chair truly belonged in my blue room right under White Buffalo Woman. Eventually, to be practical, I folded it in half over the back of the chair so I could sit in it.

I also ordered a doormat online from Zazzle.com that contained a blue and gold lotus surrounding a Flower of Life. It too wound up in a frame on my wall, too beautiful to wipe one's feet on.

As I sat on my sofa one day, looking across the room at the blank yellow wall (all the walls in the house were yellow except the bedrooms) I knew I needed one more framed picture. I had seen a free online photo some time ago called Blue Rays. This blue sun held meaning for me because St. Germain had told me while he was familiarizing me with the blue ray, that one of my soul aspects was a blue sun. Understand that we humans are not moving in a linear fashion from the third dimension to fourth to fifth and beyond. We have been moving from third dimension to multidimensionality. Each person has eleven other soul aspects of one oversoul like twelve spokes of a wheel. Some of these aspects might be in human form, some between embodiments, some in other dimensions, star systems or galaxies, maybe even in another universe.

Later, a bit doubtful, I mentioned it to the owner of Crystal Matrix Gallery in Mount Shasta. Using his unique gifts, he checked inwardly and told me one of my aspects was indeed a blue sun located in the Pleiades. He even told me its name. I asked a graphic artist friend to enlarge the photo for me. This spectacular blue sun soon dominated that wall, reminding me every day that I too am a blue sun and to embody that light to the best of my ability right here on Earth.

When you create your own temple of New Earth in your home, you may or may not want to represent the blue ray with blue accent pieces as I did. You will develop a color scheme that expresses your own unique experience and path. Let your guidance come from your heart, your intuition, synchronicities, and from your intention itself. Let the transformation of your home into a New Earth sanctuary be an adventure.

NOTE ABOUT CHANNELS: A channel is someone who brings messages through from a guide, ascended master, angel, or galactic being. Be discerning. If the one that is being channeled ever conveys fear, guilt, shame, or more division and separation, either that being or the unclear channel is not to be trusted. Trust yourself or seek other guidance. It is also ok to disagree with any being, no matter how exalted. Receive the guidance, but do not give your power away. One who serves the light does not want your dependency. They wish to empower you.

3

THE INNER TEMPLE

> When I was a child… My body was a wondrous creation. Based on carbon, it was solid enough to function in third dimension. Yet elements of many dimensions ran through it. Divine golden light could permeate every cell. My energy centers radiated light of many colors. I lived inside an outer shell of light, my light body that merged with my dense physical body. I was designed to be God expressing in physical matter. Joy-An Tucker, *When I Was a Child: As Given by the Cosmic Christ*

I really like sweets—chocolate chip cookies, chocolate candy bars, cake, pies. My mom loved to bake, so a dessert followed every meal. I probably associate cookies and cake with mother love and comfort. Some years ago, I learned that cane and beet sugars that are in almost everything on the grocery store shelves have actually been manipulated to be harmful and more addictive than they originally were, an early form of genetic engineering. You can do your own research on the health problems they contribute to. I also learned from a spiritual guide that such sugars can inhibit the ascension process in the way they affect our DNA.

Well, that was motivating because I definitely had an ascension intention. For two years, I actually quit eating any sugar except coconut palm sugar, maple syrup, and honey, which are safe. I became my own chocolatier even. Then I went to a potluck with an outstanding, mouth-watering lineup of desserts. I have never been an alcoholic, but I can understand how they can fall off the wagon! Since that time I have been on and off and generally a little less strict with myself. I do read every label and avoid the "bad" sugars most of the time.

We have all probably heard it said, "Your body is a temple." Most people identify with their bodies and ego personality. I know I did most of my life. And that is ok. We anchor all else that we are through our bodies. Our bodies are a precious gift, the vehicle through which we experience and exemplify the marriage of spirit and matter. So we can begin caring for our body temple by taking in only that which supports a higher vibration in every cell, whether that be food, music, books, media, conversations, and treatment by others. It means loving, respecting, feeding our bodies with nurturing compassion for its great service.

For example, many people eat meat, not realizing that everything is vibratory energy. When we humans eat meat, we are usually taking in the vibratory frequencies of the pain, fear, and suffering the animal experienced before and during slaughter. These destructive low frequencies enter every cell in our bodies along with the nutrients we think we can get only from killing and eating animals.

I too was omnivorous for most of my life until that awareness woke me up. It also blasted away any self-serving excuses to avoid compassion just because that's the way life is and everybody else does it.

There is no judgment here. It is a matter of choice and personal evolutionary timing. As we raise vibration and begin to feel more oneness or interconnection, we are simply more likely to feel reverence for all life rather than taking the lives of our animal relatives just to serve ourselves. As the body becomes more and more filled with light, a different perspective arises; and there is actually less need of the former ways of nurturance. We are able to live more and more on plants, light, and infinite prana—the pure life force energy from Creator. The body temple of New Earth is such a body. Your body is even now gradually evolving beyond its current carbon-based structure into a crystalline structure of light. How awesome to imagine that!

RECIPE FOR ECSTATIC DINING

- Eat whatever you choose.
- Chew it very slowly, about one bite per second or slower
- Focus your full attention toward the back of your tongue, noticing nuances of flavor and texture, feeling gratitude for the life force energy.
- If your mind starts running, your chewing will become fast again, so refocus.
- Notice the sensation flowing from the back of your tongue down to your heart center, solar plexus and the rest of your body.
- Delicious!

The inner temple is more than our physical bodies, more than our personality selves and our names. If you are reading this book, you already know or have an inkling that you are more than that. You may already know or feel that your body is surrounded by layers of energy called the emotional, mental, and spiritual bodies. And you extend even beyond those. The energy field around a person, often called the aura, can be close and contracted or as big as the earth itself and beyond. It can be dark or smoky or as radiant as a sun and all gradations of color in between. We humans start to wake up or evolve when we realize we are more than our body identity and personality. Then we each begin to explore, to seek to understand our potential greatness, our divinity, which includes our body temple.

What is this I AM that Yeshua and other Masters mention? It is one of the names given to the individualized aspect of Creator connected to every human body. Every time you say the powerful words, "I am", you are Creator creating your reality in that moment. According to ascended master teachings, this part of yourself is also the eternal real you. It exists above your head in another dimension and looks like a sun surrounded by a rainbow of the seven rays. Below your God presence, is your higher self, also called the Christ self. Your higher self is eternal and already in oneness or enlightened. It is your connecting link to your I AM. Your I AM surrounds the body with a tube of light and anchors in each heart. Our job is to bring this Divine presence fully into our bodies, so that we are that. To illustrate, I found this chart:

Chart of Your Divine Self, used by kind permission of The Summit Lighthouse, www.SummitLighthouse.org. All rights reserved.

Imagine that sun, your I AM God Presence, sliding down your tube of light all the way into your heart and filling your body. That suggestion came from my inner child! It works.

Here is one way of using the creative power of your I AM:

PRANA PLAY for receiving life force energy

Originally taught by St. Germain through Ashamarae McNamara

(Prana, chi, qi, life force energy are all names for the same thing)

After eating half of your usual size meal or during a fast and with a glass of water near

1. Become aware that you have an I AM God presence and below that, your Higher Self or Christ Self, also called your Buddha Nature.
2. As in the picture, visualize these aspects of yourself and your physical body enveloped in a tube of light. It you can't visualize it, jut trust that these aspects of you are always there.
3. Say commandingly, "I AM the resurrection and the life of pranic energy in my body"
4. Feel the pranic energy, the life force gathering in your stomach and radiating into your body. You will likely feel more full.
5. Hold the glass of water and say, "I AM the resurrection and the life of pranic energy in this water."
6. Blow into the water and drink it.
7. Note how you feel.

Just as in the outer home we have much junk, debris, furniture, clothes, knick knacks that are no longer needed in our more elegant, clean, and high frequency temple of New Earth, so also this clearing of worn out, unserviceable beliefs, conditioning, behaviors, thought patterns, habits of judgment and criticism, competition, lack consciousness, victim consciousness—and you get the idea—becomes the work of every evolutionary path. I had to stop patterns of judgment, criticism, lack consciousness, and holding on as part of the process of getting rid of bedbugs (with the help of professional pest control, which might be likened at another level to a psychologist or spiritual counselor). I threw out a lot of household goods to make way for my Temple of New Earth. The outer reflects the inner.

It's not just about letting go of that which is no longer supportive of one's personal growth, evolution, and ascension: it is about replacing it with something more harmonious, radiant, beautiful, joyful, loving—a higher vibration inner and outer.

RECIPE FOR GRATITUDE, A HIGHER VIBRATION

- One glass of water or any liquid drink
- One gold fizzy capsule (imagined) filled with gratitude
- Drop the capsule into your water and allow it to fizz.
- At the same time, notice the feeling in your body, especially your heart center. No effort is needed.

Do this every time you drink anything. My inner child invented this alchemy, and it works.

4

LETTING GO: EASIER SAID THAN DONE?

St Germain doesn't mess around. No you poor girl from him. No pity—but great compassion. When I became stuck on a previous hamster wheel a few years ago, I became sick of my own mental snarl and complaining snarliness.

"St Germain," I said. I don't want to feel like this all the time, but this neighbor is really mean. I get angry every time I walk up the road past his neighboring property and every time I irrigate my fields. He takes more than his share of water and yells aggressively at me when I try to talk to him."

I started to tell the story of my woes, but he stopped me. "No more story," he said. Drop the stories. Free yourself." He continued, " You are here on Earth to learn compassion—in this case, compassion for his loneliness, separation, unconsciousness. Compassion for the suffering he has experienced in his life to make him so unfriendly, so full of hate and anger. Forgive him and thank him for this opportunity to develop your compassion." (St. Germain through Ashamarae McNamara)

I had told St. Germain about the mini stroke I had had a week before. This was the lesson I had to learn if I wanted to prevent the big one, which was otherwise headed my way.

Darn, there it was again. I had to let go of my own anger and self-righteousness and forgive this dude. And thank him on top of that! The possibility of another stroke provided great motivation, however, and with St. Germain there, supporting me and filling me with his pure love and compassion, it was not so hard. I began to feel compassion and forgiveness, which felt so much better than the other attitude. No way I wanted to go back. I also loved how compassion felt in my own body, especially my heart. It was as if my compassion was for me at the same time. I even appreciated that my neighbor loved his land, spending long hours mowing his fields of grass and caring for his irrigation ditches. They were all he had, and they were not even his, for he worked for the absentee landowner.

When we make the shift from one attitude to another of higher vibration, such as compassion or gratitude—that is letting go.

There are also beliefs about reality we must release, especially in a world that has been so mind controlled by mass media, the agendas of the powerful, and manipulation by religious dogma. Letting go of what no longer serves often requires believing only what our hearts affirm as true and in alignment with love, non-judgment, harmony and unity—the way of New Earth.

- Before you let go of a belief, thought, or feeling, you gain more wisdom if you first acknowledge it.

- Second, thank it for its service to your survival, protection, or comfort in your life, understanding that it no longer serves your highest good or the highest good of all.

- Third, forgive yourself for any harm that your beliefs, thoughts, feelings, words or actions toward yourself or others may have caused.

- Fourth, forgive the other. Then you can actually let go rather than suppress or stuff it or add more judgment. You know that forgiveness is complete when you can feel love and compassion for the other.

St Germain has said that when Mary Magdalene stood before the cross, she was able to forgive even the Roman soldier who was torturing her beloved. And Yeshua himself showed the way when he said, "Forgive them, Lord, for they know not what they do." (from the Bible, many translations)

- Fifth, ask that what you are releasing be transmuted to the highest vibration of love.

- Sixth, replace it. Fill your body, mind, and spirit with higher vibratory thoughts, feelings, words, and actions. Focus on creating and being what you really want and who you really are. Transformation is about both emptying and filling. It means letting go of the old and replacing it with that which will support your higher aspirations and visions.

As you create your Temple of New Earth, you may want to display an image of Quan Yin, Mother Mary, Mary Magdalene or any other being who is a master of love and compassion. Beyond displaying her image as a reminder, ask her to fill you with her frequencies so that you can become familiar with them and anchor them in your own body.

To make it even simpler, here is another way of letting go by using the power of intention.

1) <u>Set the intention</u> to release any conditioning, limiting beliefs, emotions, attitudes that no longer serve. If you can be specific, that's good. Often, however, these energies are unconscious or difficult to articulate. Here is a short list of examples of limiting beliefs:

Not good enough.

Don't deserve it.

Not enough.

Not worthy.

Powerless.

Life is suffering.

One has to suffer to be spiritual.

Bodies are only matter.

People are only their bodies and personality.

Humans have only one life.

Existence ends at death

2) As you inhale, tense every area of your entire body as tightly as you can, including your face and head.

3) Exhale and relax all tension with the <u>intention</u> of releasing all that no longer

serves a higher vibratory state.

4) Keep repeating until you feel complete for now and do this practice each day as needed.

(This short, sweet method was shared by the Arcturians through Natalie Glasson at omna.org) The Arcturians are an enlightened galactic civilization.

5

GOLDEN TREASURES

The yellow ray and gold ray are also emanations from Source: one the Ray of Divine Wisdom, connecting with God mind; the other the Flame of Resurrection. The gold ray is one of the rays that Yeshua radiated and anchored on Earth. It is also called the light of the Cosmic Christ, who guided Yeshua during his last embodiment. A Christ is one who is enlightened, in oneness with Source and all creation. Every human comes into embodiment with one or two predominant color frequency rays, the colors in a rainbow. Each then must master all seven rays as part of his or her journey to ascension. Now there are five additional rays as well. The gold ray is the twelfth ray.

One of my rooms was already full of gold accents and golden light. The wisdom ray already existed in my cheerful yellow walls and ceilings throughout the house. This room was an extension of my dining room in my open floor plan house. It contained a Chinese gold brocade wall hanging picturing graceful white cranes about to take flight and an oriental screen painting of cherry blossoms and bamboo against a gold background. Both of these were elegant decor I had inherited from my mother. I had thrown out a mustard gold corduroy recliner that I had bought some years before for a few dollars at a yard sale. I kept one comfortable goldish-tan plush chair graced by a round glass side table with four gold legs. Each leg was topped by a pinecone shape, which represents the pineal gland, the connecting link in our brains to higher consciousness. It is a physical part of our crown chakra. This little table became a medicine wheel of crystals with a blown glass figurine of Mother Mary, representing the Divine Feminine, in the center. Behind her rose a graceful white orchid in a golden vase. I had found this glorious plant in a Raley's grocery store when I was looking for bananas. The gold vase clinched the decision and I carried it to the checkout counter without regard for price.

A round gold wicker laundry basket with a lid became a table holding a green plant. Likewise, a plant with green fronds sat behind and above the oriental screen. It looked as if live bamboo leaves were growing out of the screen.

Hmm. The above picture shows that a larger plant is needed in the right corner to balance the left. Would you agree?

On another level I filled and surrounded my home with golden light every day. Visitors could feel the good energy when they walked in. You too can fill your body and home with golden light. The frequencies that you radiate into your house are the most valuable part of your creation.

I spent several days looking online for a gold area rug to enhance the gold ray room. I saw some I liked but they were made of polypropylene. One day my inner guidance, which I was listening to more respectfully these days, said clearly "Search for a gold flower of life rug." I immediately wrote in the search terms, and voila! A beautiful round gold flower of life rug was the first thing I saw. It was made of polyester and cotton and being marketed on Etsy. I ordered it enthusiastically.

When I received the rug, it was thinner than most rugs and, with a diameter of about five feet, too small for the intended area. Instead I placed it in front of my iron stove between the dining area and gold accented living area. It was really all one room anyway because of the open floor plan. It was perfect there, both decorative and meaningful, for the flower of life reflects harmony and balance in its sacred geometry. It is also called the Seed of Life because it represents the early stages of a growing embryo. It was a metaphor for my creation of a New Earth sanctuary and a global movement to bring New Earth home.

I so liked my unicorn tapestry in the blue ray room that I wanted an angel tapestry to hang above my fake-wood iron stove in the dining area. Fire danger was not an issue because I no longer burned propane in it. It's amazing how many angel throws are for sale. But none was quite right. Finally I found one called Holiday Angel from Bed, Bath, and Beyond by textile artist Lena Liu. It was threaded with dark gold and rust gold and artfully depicted a female angel standing in front of a pillar-lined temple stair, bending gracefully to feed the doves gathered around her. The whole scene radiated the divine feminine energy that I wanted in my Temple of New Earth, for in this now time the Divine Mother brings female balance to the masculine on this planet once again.

Golden Treasures

In truth, the form of Creator of this Universe, the magnificent consciousness whose body is the Great Central Sun of the universe, and Prime Source beyond that have no gender, for all is contained within her heart and being. Divine Mother has merged her energies with our Earth to assist Earth's ascension and all life on the planet to bring New Earth to fruition. (In the English language "she" and "her" contain "he", so that is the pronoun I most often use in this book.)

The angel tapestry, like Divine Mother, exemplified gentleness, grace, tenderness, love, and compassion. The gold flower of life in front of the fireplace and the golden angel tapestry above it together made an uplifting, impactful sight. A carved wood Buddha, sitting solidly in meditation, a hand raised in blessing, completed the scene with his calm equanimity and balanced harmony. He represents the divine masculine.

During one session with Ascended Master St. Germain, he enabled us to anchor a flower of life in every chakra (energy center) of our bodies, including the hands and feet, so that we would literally embody the harmony and balance of this geometric form. After that, as sometimes happens in spiritual psychological work, everything disharmonious in my psyche came forward in the next few months to be acknowledged and cleared or released. I needed help!

I got it. I asked for it and the assistance arrived. A channel named Natalie Glasson, founder of the Sacred School of Omna, brought forth a teaching from Yeshua (Jesus). He shared that during his life on Earth, he would sometimes get angry or discouraged by the ignorance and circumstances in his world. He dealt with it by picturing himself as a character outside himself, and he would just listen to that part of himself express his thoughts and feelings. Then he would forgive and embrace that part of himself as well as the triggering circumstances. I tried that technique, which worked wonderfully. Often we just need to be heard, if only by ourselves.

Yeshua also described how the challenges of his life sometimes made him feel separate from God or filled him with doubt about his mission. Then he would allow himself to "fall" into God to regain his state of oneness. Even as he spoke through his messenger, I felt myself falling into God in complete relaxation and surrender. The result was an infilling of indescribable peace and love as I fell deep into my heart. Now it is a frequent practice until I can be in that state of oneness 24/7.

Call on Yeshua yourself, and ask him to help you fall into God. Have no expectations. Do nothing. Just allow. Surrender

On Divine New Earth all humanity and all creatures great and small exist in that loving, creative oneness, that unity with Creator. Every creation and manifestation arises from that state of being. Imagine that. Imagine how you feel as you create and live in your own New Earth home.

If you need assistance with your God merge, call upon Yeshua/Jesus or your own favorite master, angel, or teacher of light. They are all one together on the inner planes of consciousness, and they are all advancing the same Divine Plan for the ascension of humanity and Mother Earth. (You can even call on me, but use email or phone!) They are always ready to assist; but to respect your free will, by divine law they can assist only when they are heartfully asked.

GOLD LIGHT ALCHEMY

1. Breathe slowly and deeply at least three times, relaxing all parts of your body with each breath.
2. Feel or imagine a warm, sparkling, golden light in your heart center in the middle of your chest.
3. Allow that warm sparkling golden light to expand throughout your body, filling every cell with golden sparkles.
4. Allow that warm sparkling golden light to expand all around your body into your aura.
5. Allow that golden light to fill the room you are in.
6. Allow the golden light to expand into and around your whole house.
7. Focus back in your heart.
8. Feel your feet on the ground, your seat on the chair, wiggle your fingers and toes as you become fully aware of your body.

6

GREEN GRASS AND A STROKE OF LUCK

Every blade of grass holds not only Gaia but also stars and heavens. —St Germain

Several years ago I was throwing hay over the fence to my horses when I suddenly felt dizzy and unbalanced. Sometimes such symptoms can be caused by the acceleration of frequencies on the planet. However, I intuitively felt my condition might not be so benign. I managed to get back into my house a short distance away and told my housemate I might be having a stroke. Could she look up the symptoms on the internet please and take me to the hospital if necessary.

As I lay on the couch waiting for her, I called Archangel Raphael and Ascended Master Hilarion, both masters of the healing green ray. I imagined emerald green light pouring into my head as I asked for assistance. Immediately I felt more relaxed, less anxious, confident that all would be well.

At the hospital I was told I had indeed had a transient ischemic attack, a mini stroke. I giggled when I could not touch two index fingers together and missed my nose entirely when I aimed for it. I also had lost feeling on my right side, which I noticed most in my fingers and inside my mouth, The doctor gave me an aspirin and told me to wait an hour before going home. I felt quite at ease in the light of the green ray, and my symptoms soon passed except in my fingers and mouth.

I chose to view this whole experience as a stroke of luck, for a few days later in a conversation with St Germain described earlier, he advised me of its cause as already described—habits of judgment and criticism which in turn created physical disharmony—and enabled me to avoid a more serious stroke down the line. Instead it served as a wake up call.

I love nature's green—my irrigated green pastures; elm, sycamore, and cottonwood trees lush with green leaves; the green pine and fir forests on the mountains all around; and kale, chard, and spinach in my garden.

Nature is full of green and other natural frequencies since every color is a vibratory frequency. Nature is the best place to go for healing (without the accompaniment of cell phones) I am grateful that I can access nature by stepping out my door. And it is so worth the effort to travel even further afield if necessary.

Green Grass and a Stroke of Luck

Nature indoors and outdoors.

We can also bring nature indoors as you probably already do. Potted green plants and flowers enhance the energy in every home and certainly belong in your own temple of New Earth. Every room in my house now contains plants. The green ray is also represented in my gold room, which is graced with large and small green plants and one of two green and gold papasan accent chairs. Eventually I will keep both papasans in the dining room and find another perfect chair for the gold room. Nothing need be static.

Two green and gold papasan chairs in dining room

A forest green tablecloth dresses up the round wooden table in the adjacent dining room. It's amazing how much difference a tablecloth can make over a scratched brown wooden table.

Dining table backed by kitchen

It seems to anchor and unite the qualities of green in the combined space, creating flow. The gold chairs do the same with the gold qualities. Of course that room also contains the sage green wall-to-wall carpet that runs through the whole house.

My gold ray room combined with my green accented dining room, graced by the life force energy of green plants, is uplifting and full of light, and I love to sit in any part of it as I bring light into my body, then radiate it into the room, the whole house, the town, the state, the country, and finally to the whole Earth. Imagine doing that yourself in your own space of love.

If you want to vitalize, cleanse, and help heal your body, call for the healing green ray.

GREEN RAY PLAY

1. Call for the presence and assistance of Archangel Raphael and Ascended Master Hilarion if you would like.
2. Breathe into your heart until you feel calm and relaxed.
3. Visualize emerald green light with gold sparkles coming from above into your crown as if you had a hole in the top of your head.
4. Let if fill your head and flow down to fill your heart center, including your actual heart.
5. From your heart let it flow into your arteries and throughout your vascular system as your blood becomes emerald green light.
6. With great love for your body, let the light flow from your blood into all your cells, tissue, organs, nerves and bone.
7. Enjoy the feeling and appreciate your body.
8. Wiggle your fingers and toes as you become fully present in your body.

7

PURPLE MOUNTAIN MAJESTY

Transmute, transmute
By violet fire
All causes and cores
Not of God's desire.
I AM a being of cause alone
That cause is love
The sacred tone

—Patricia Cota Robles

One day as I did my laundry, I noticed an object between my dryer and the wall. Pulling it out, I was astounded to see an acrylic photo print of Mt Shasta bathed in purple light, as it sometimes appears when the pink evening alpine glow merges into night. I am sure it was also photo shopped a bit to emphasize the violet quality.

This was obviously meant to be an anonymous gift, but I knew who had sneaked it into my house. The culprit was a man who sometimes cared for my vegetable garden and with whom I occasionally had tea and conversation at the Black Bear Gallery in Mt Shasta. I had seen and admired the pricey photo in the gallery on one of those occasions. I knew him to be generous and helpful to many people even though he lived inconspicuously in a tiny one-bedroom apartment in the middle of town. When I next saw him, I told him all about finding the purple mountain in my laundry room as if I did not know who had left it there.

With delight I hung the photo against the white wall in my bedroom, my violet ray room.

Purple Mountain Majesty

In that room was a violet and tan wool rug from India that I had found at an estate sale years ago. I had moved it from another room where it no longer belonged. The moment I had laid it on the floor, I knew this was to be the violet ray room. On another wall was a print of the fifth dimensional solar violet flame from eraofpeace.org (shown in chapter 8) all connecting colorfully with my bedspread printed with pink and violet roses.

When I stand before this purple picture of Mt Shasta or in view of the mountain itself, I merge with her, feeling Source energies pouring down through her peak and through the crown of my head at the same time, then radiating from my heart center into the world. You too can do this with a picture of the mountain or the next time you visit.

People sometimes refer fondly to St. Germain as the purple man. When he appeared on Mt Shasta to a hiker named Guy Ballard in the 1930's to begin his teachings, one of the most important and repeated lessons was the use of the violet flame or ray to transmute low vibrational, discordant, and harmful energies in oneself and the environment. Nearly a hundred years later, in 2022 for example, lightworkers all over the world who had learned this lesson were pouring violet light or violet fire into and around the earth to transmute and clear the fear, chaos, and control agendas that seemed to prevail in the outer world.

Sometimes people had judgments about what they were clearing; but loving, non-judgmental neutrality—often called divine neutrality—is the best approach. The violet flame contains not only the frequencies of transmutation, but also of love, forgiveness, and tenderness. Imagine violet tenderness pouring through yourself to the world. The color violet is actually a blend of pink and blue—love and power, the power of love.

Once St Germain recommended visualizing a food blender filled with violet light, putting that which we wanted to transmute into the blender, then turning it on! (St. Germain has a sense of humor.) I also use the violet flame to clear old energies attached to used furniture.

Since I was getting up in age a bit, St Germain taught me a way to upgrade my brain with violet light. He said it would also help deter dementia and Alzheimers. I share it with you here so that you too may use it and share it with others. It is good for anyone old enough to follow the instructions.

VIOLET LIGHT BRAIN UPGRADE

1. Ask Ascended Master St Germain to be present and to assist you. You might want to have someone read this to you slowly as you follow.
2. Close your eyes and focus on your breath as your mind becomes more quiet. Continue until your mind is calmer.
3. Breath directly into your brain. Inhale and exhale in and out of your brain. Use your will to help you focus.
4. Ask your higher self to increase the current in your brain.
5. See within the brain the most brilliant violet light pulsating through this current.
6. See your brain like a blazing violet sun through the increasing current.
7. ....BREATHE...
8. Breathe brilliant violet light from the brain stem down your spine to your coccyx bone (tailbone), up and down, up and down. Your spinal fluid for the moment becomes liquid violet light. Feel this with your entire being. It will improve your motor function.
9. Breath deeply with your whole body 3X
10. Open your eyes and keep your body still.

11. Anchor into your whole body with your breath.

12. Move your fingers, toes, and body gently

13. Note how you feel and function during the next week

After he taught this healing practice to me, he explained that a cause of dementia and Alzheimers is exposure to violence, whether real or fictional as on TV or video games. The brain does not know the difference. Watching violence decreases brain function.

Other ways to increase brain function are comedy that does not diminish another, movies in which people help each other, music that lifts the heart, hugging and touching in a tender way, and dancing. Raise frequencies in your self and home with this understanding. With strong intention, also fill your home and self with violet light or violet flames to clear energies that do not fit your vision of love and harmony.

8

PINK PYRAMID

I grew up in a house filled with beige furniture, a beige wall-to-wall carpet, and beige walls. My beautiful mother usually wore beige clothes. Maybe that's why I never became an artist and never paid much attention to color other than to have preferences for some more than others in my environment and clothes. On the other hand, when it was time for me to attend an interview with an agent of Radcliffe College during my senior year in high school, my mom bought me a full-skirted purple jumper and a pink blouse to wear to the meeting. A couple of weeks later, I received a letter from the agent saying that although I qualified academically, the sophisticated women at Radcliffe would eat me for breakfast.

Now in addition to containing violet accents, my bedroom contains pink in the tea roses on my bedspread, a pink comforter, pink sheets, and the pink mane and tail of my plush toy unicorn.

Pleiadians in a group called Laarkmaa, from an enlightened extraterrestrial civilization, first introduced me to color rays, particularly pink. They asked us to radiate the pink ray of divine love around and into Earth. Since the activity was new to me at that time, it was a struggle at first. I performed the service with my mind, enveloping Earth with pink light from a space-high vantage point, but I did not feel it. One day Laarkmaa asked the group to feel the love, to qualify the color with love. Even then I was still in my mind trying to feel it.

A few years later, in a class with St. Germain, he asked us to invite Mother Mary into our presence and to feel her love, receive her love. That was a truly palpable experience. When Mother Mary is present, love is all there is. When one feels the love of a master pouring in, the frequency is unmistakable. Thereafter, I was able to truly feel in my heart the love frequency of pink light. Better yet, I learned the blissful feeling of being a conduit of that love, rather than the sole generator.

Ascended Master Mary, mother of Yeshua, heads the Sisterhood of the Rose, which includes female ascended masters such as Mary Magdalene, Quan Yin, Isis, Hathor, Lady Portia, Tara, White Buffalo Woman. Each of these is the twin of a male ascended master since ascension requires the union of the male and female aspects of a human. Many ordinary extraordinary women around the world have also been initiated into the Sisterhood of the Rose. Men are also welcome, just as women are welcome in the Brotherhood of Light. At the level of mastery, all are one.

A few days after I wrote the paragraph above, I browsed through Soul Connections, a store in Mt Shasta. In a rack of art prints of various ascended masters and angels, one especially caught my attention: an exquisite print of Mother Mary, dressed in a pink robe, shining with pink light and rainbows, fronted by a pink rose. The night before I had been imagining a pink rose picture of some kind above my bed. Although it was not what I thought I came in to buy, it is what I left with. Now I am blessed by beautiful Ascended Mother Mary above the head of my bed.

Pink Pyramid

Mother Mary, the 5D Solar Violet Flame, and Uni

Although I cannot initiate you here, I can assist your attunement to the Sisterhood and the pink ray of love. Have with you a pink quartz crystal and a pink rose if possible. (Keep a crystal in every room of your house) You can do this sitting or lying in bed if you like.

1. Breathe into your heart until you feel peaceful and centered there.
2. Call forth a four-sided pyramid of pink, crystalline, sparkling light to form around you.
3. Ask Mother Mary to be with you. Feel her presence and receive her frequencies of infinite nurturing love. Ask all the masters of the Sisterhood of the Rose to surround you, and feel their loving, supporting, powerful presence even if you don't know them all.
4. See or imagine your pyramid filled with pink sparkly light.
5. Let the sparkly pink light fill your heart, your body, all your cells.
6. Let the light flow through you into Mother Earth to ground and anchor these energies.

Another wonderful way to use the pink ray of love is with your partner or any loved one, including your children.

Sit facing each other.

Take turns sending a pink ray from your crown to your partner' crown. The receiver does nothing but receive.

Send a pink ray from your third eye chakra (in the middle of your forehead a bit above your eyebrows. Take turns.

Send a pink ray from your hearts, each in turn.

If you do not have a partner, imagine doing the same with an ascended master of your choice, with your own higher self, or with your twin flame, whom you may never have met. Call that one forth, and see, feel or trust that he/she is there.

RECIPE for PINK LIGHT LEMONADE

Add ½ squeezed lemon, 1 tsp. or more of maple syrup, and an optional drop of red berry juice to a glass of water. Imagine your water filled with sparkling pink light. Or just add the pink light to plain water. Drink the liquid pink light. You can do this with any of the rays.

9

SLIDING INTO WHITE

White was just white in my house until I changed my perspective of colors. Whenever I look at the white walls in the bedrooms, white doors and trim, white accents here and there, or a white refrigerator, I now choose to remember the white ray of purity, at least some of the time. I imagine the white sparkling diamond ascension ray of purity shining down from my I AM, my God presence, into and around my body, purifying all four lower bodies—physical, mental, emotional, and spiritual—purifying, purifying, purifying. We need purification every day unless we live in a cave with a rock over the entrance. I recommend it. Not only does it feel good; it is also a part of the ascension process that Yeshua demonstrated in his life on Earth. And now it is your turn—if you choose.

My white orchid is my favorite reminder of the white ray. It radiates living purity in its simple beauty. It is divine perfection personified (or plantified). What heart's joy it is to look at a white orchid and breathe it in with so much appreciation. It feeds me through my eyes.

A shift of perspective can change our world. When we look at ordinary things in our lives—people, colors, trees, animals, space—and see instead the wondrous divine beauty in such things, then we are seeing the world as a master sees and feels. Then we are getting a glimpse of enlightenment, feeling the Christing within. It takes so little effort, just a choice really. Anyone can do it. To see and feel the holiness in your own home, just by a little inner shift, transforms your relationship to everything in your surroundings. Start with just once a day, then more and more often until the new perspective is your reality, your truth, THE truth.

My kitchen has a large skylight through which light pours. It is like the crown chakra of my house. And my appliances are white. Whether you have a skylight or not, imagine white light pouring into your kitchen. Just for fun when I am wearing socks, I love to run a couple of steps and slide into the light like a kid. It's one fun way I raise vibration. To play it safe, I don't recommend that to anyone, but let your inner child out and do it in your imagination.

OK, that may sound a bit silly, yet play. Don't take yourself too seriously. The purity, trust, innocence and joy of a child are a key to the New Earth. Be in that trust and innocence with the white ray or any of the other colors at least once a day. Let a color remind you of the ray and imagine it coming down through and around your body. Notice how it feels.

An ascended master named Serapis Bey is the master of the white ray in charge of every individual's ascension process when a person is ready to focus on that. The crystals associated with the white ray are quartz and diamonds, so grace your house with clear or white quartz crystals, conscious of their purpose. Even if you aren't interested in ascension yet in your evolution, invite into you and your surroundings the white ray of purity for health and well-being.

If ascension sounds scary or too far fetched for you, be aware that ascension at this time in our evolution does not mean ascending out of the body or even with the body, disappearing into another realm all by yourself. It means ascending INTO your upgraded body temple, your God presence fully embodied, leading the way in all that you say and do. It means being of continued service and example to the rest of awakening humanity until all who choose can move upwards and onwards together in unity. Meanwhile, our Earth is accelerating her frequencies, and we will enjoy the ride a lot more if we keep up.

10

BATHROOM BREAK

Go ahead and laugh. I am too. I mentioned white light in the kitchen. Now it's time for a bathroom break.

During one Zoom class with St. Germain through messenger Ashamarae, this amazing ascended master shocked and surprised all of us. Looking at us with all his love, he began talking to us about how we poo! The teaching was serious and hilarious at the same time and, of course, occurred on more than one level. He went into outrageous detail about how we need to be patient, not force or push, let the natural movements of the bowel do the job. And eat more fruit, drink more water. The adult audience responded like a bunch of giggly embarrassed seventh-graders.

A Buddhist monk, Chogyam Trungpa Rinpoche, who founded a secular Buddhist spiritual path called Shambhala Warrior Training, described how when he was a child his teachers made him sit up straight on the toilet, stay conscious, connect to his Buddha nature, and continue keeping a quiet mind.

In my guest bathroom I have a small framed engraving of a lovely seated angel, arms open, ecstatically receiving an influx of light into her heart. It hangs on the wall in front of the toilet. Even when we sit on our thrones, we can be the conscious connecting link between heaven and earth, spirit and matter. When I sit on that particular throne, the angel is my mirror and my reminder, plus it makes me chuckle at my projection. This angel shows that receiving Creator energies into self is not a mental experience. It is a full body experience. When you open your whole body and being to light and love, you can feel the joyful bliss in every cell.

I am also fortunate to have a large carpeted master bathroom. On one of two side-by-side dressers, I established an altar, which includes a picture of Mother Mary looking lovingly at a bouquet of roses like a babe in her arms. The roses represent the souls of humanity. When I look at it, I too imagine that I am holding humanity in my arms with gentle love. The original painting, *The Souls of Humanity*, was created by artist Velvalee after a workshop at The Stargate Experience Academy in Mt. Shasta, and prints are available from The Stargate Experience Inc. She had never painted before.

On the counter next to my sink I keep an orchid; and a colorful runner draped over a shelf adds a touch of vibrant reds, yellows, greens, blues, violet—all the rainbow colors. It is a room I enjoy walking into.

The point is everything is spiritual. Nothing is out of bounds. Everything is a mirror for us to learn and grow from. These examples here provide a metaphor for life in general. So, in your own home sanctuary, pay attention to your bathroom. Is it already beautiful? Would you like to make it so? Does it contain a plant, a flower, some wall art? Matching rugs and a toilet seat cover are attractive touches if you don't already have them. Do you stay conscious of your divinity while seated on your throne? Do you appreciate your wondrous body? Do you allow a proper poo?

PART 2

SACRED GEOMETRY, SOUND, SPACE

11

CIRCLES, CURVES, AND LIGHTSHIPS

In Feng Sui décor, circles and curves are desirable for softening straight lines and angles and for enabling energy to move more freely and smoothly in any space. I intuitively liked to do that anyway even without being an expert in Feng Sui. In one corner of my gold room, for example, I had placed a round wicker basket/table with a plant on it. Another corner I modified with an oriental screen with a plant above it, its palm-like fronds curving over the painted scene. Together they turned two ninety degree corners into a curve.

The Flower of Life rug was a circle as was my dining room table. The two papasan chairs added more circles; and whenever possible I placed chairs at an angle in corners to round out a room. A round, wood, marble-topped lamp table broke up the straight line of one wall of my blue room. In my perspective, circles and curves add a feminine feel to a room as well as softening lines and angles

Find the curves

As you create your own temple, play with circles and curves. Notice how they make you feel. Notice how they change the energy or feel of a room.

Circles and curves also relate to our thinking patterns. For example, a writer can circle around an idea, looking at it from many perspectives; or a writer may start with a thesis and proceed in a linear fashion to prove or expound on that thesis. Logical linear thought has a feel and purpose different from intuitive, creative, non-linear thinking. Both are needed in balance.

Having spent quite a few years in linear, logical academia in my twenties, I have had to learn to pay attention to and trust intuition. One book that effectively demonstrates that way of being is the second volume of *Adventures of a Western Mystic*, by Peter Mt Shasta. The author worked closely with St Germain, and, following his inner guidance, had some amazing adventures in the school of life. Intuition in the moment often works better than using one's mind to figure out every detail ahead of time. We all have something called heart mind, which is much more expansive and wise than our brain minds. Now when I have a decision to make or want to know something, I first ask my heart.

Circles and spheres also represent wholeness, inclusiveness, and unity of all parts within the whole. Unity and inclusiveness are the opposite of separation and division, which we are leaving behind. There is no us and them; this religion or that; this political party or that; unacceptable skin colors, or hair colors, or races; or if you have one view or affiliation, you can't include another. The New Earth is all-inclusive because it is not about beliefs and dogmas; it is about individuals who are one with Creator and each other, all expressing the creativity, wisdom, love, joy, and laughter of Mother/Father God in their own unique ways.

Likewise, as humans create New Earth in collaboration with the Light Realms, including the enlightened galactic civilizations, each will contribute according to his or her special interests, passions, skills, and talents. As you create your self and your home to be New Earth sanctuaries, you too will do it in your own unique, inspired way, according to your Divine plan, evolutionary path, and sense of decoration and design—that which makes your heart sing. The difference between just decorating your home and creating a temple or sanctuary of New Earth is intention, conscious purpose, and holding high vibrational states such as love, joy, peace, harmony and compassion.

There are other forms of sacred geometry you may want to include in your home as well. Both in my living room and next to my bed I have a four-sided pyramid shaped salt lamp. Pyramids are a powerful geometry. Small and large ones have a healing, vitalizing effect on everything around them. From Ascended Master Sananda, another name for the ascended aspect of Jesus, I learned a practice called the diamond heart. In this practice you imagine a four-sided pyramid in your heart center. Call in your favorite guide such as Sananda or Buddha. Sit quietly in the center of this pyramid for a while. Look around you. Feel and listen. It will be your unique experience. Then see a shining multifaceted diamond somewhere in that space. Feel that too. Merge with it. It is the Divine presence in your heart.

Another sacred geometry is a six-pointed star, which represents, among other things, male and female balance. It is an upward pointing triangle combined with a downward pointing triangle. In its multidimensional form it is also a MerKaBa vehicle used for traveling across dimensions or for healing. After St. Germain activated our MerKaBa's—which everyone has—and encouraged us to practice with them for twenty-one days, I asked him what they were good for. He said those two things, healing and travel, were all he could share with me for now. After those twenty-one days, I began inviting people who agreed to receive such healings into my MerKaBa field and watched as their etheric (non-physical energy) bodies transformed before my inner eyes. This activity was all at a distance, and I never told someone exactly when the healing was going to happen. Reported results were quite amazing. Each person profoundly felt the light and higher vibrations as well as at least partial physical and emotional healings. One woman was in such pain that she wanted to die. After the MerKaBa healing, her pain was gone. I was as surprised and delighted as she was.

The flying saucer shape that we associate with space travel is a spinning MerKaBa field operated and directed by intention. As for my own MerKaBa lightship travel, I have tried a bit of that and am still learning. I prefer just to travel in consciousness for now until I have more confidence. For fun here is a saucer cloud photo that I took one sunrise from my own back yard.

12

MANDELBROT, ANYONE?

Brot is the German word for bread, and the Mandelbrot set, which is a mathematical equation, is something delicious to chew on for sure.

In the 1990's, crop circles were appearing overnight all over Great Britain and elsewhere as well. These designs cut out in wheat or barley fields started out simple and became very complex over the years, impossible to call a hoax. It is unlikely they were made by ordinary humans, but their origins were unclear and the subject of much speculation and controversy.

When I first saw crop designs illustrating Mandelbrot sets, I was astounded and intrigued. These crop designs had to be messages from advanced galactic civilizations. Each one seemed to be a code and a teaching that bypassed the logical mind. The sacred geometry of replication described mathematically by a man named Mandelbrot spoke directly to my heart knowing. Each piece of mysterious field art that illustrated the Mandelbrot concept had a central design that replicated over and over again, like the waves in the shell of a nautilus. These replicate offshoots were called fractals.

My further research found that such recurring patterns are found throughout nature. The Flower of Life is one of these. As I write at my dining room table, a Christmas cactus sits in the center. Every leaf replicates the one it is attached to—just one immediate example. The biggest crop circle was 450 meters in diameter and illustrated nature's pattern of creation:

Fractal Crop Circle, Science.org, 8/20/2001

So why did I get all excited about Mandelbrot sets back then? It set off a light bulb in my brain. If humans are said to be made in the image of God, maybe there is something to that idea. Then each human is a replica of God. Somewhere along the way, people got it backwards, thinking that God looks like a man—an old fearsome, judgmental patriarch. But no, the form of the loving, nonjudgmental Creator of everything in this universe is the Great Central Sun, the body of a grand, conscious, infinitely loving being. Beyond that is a Creator of multiverses. (My mind was expanding to the limit!) Each emanation of Creator starts a cascade of replicas ad infinitum right into the density of the third dimension. Each human is therefore a replica of God, I reasoned.

That thought made me want to laugh and leap around. I am a fractal, a sun of God! Oh boy! That makes so much sense! My physical body is a coat over the real me! A sun! And I can have all the God wisdom and love and other qualities too if I can let that part of me shine!

The little me in a human body reasserted itself again, of course, but that revelation inspired by a Mandelbrot set crop circle has been a foundation and guiding light on my spiritual journey. Therefore, a picture of this crop circle had to have a place in my Temple of New Earth, but not on the wall this time. I learned while rug shopping that a rug maker like the one that made the flower of life carpet can make a rug from any photo. I still needed a rug for the larger part of my gold room. This crop circle would be perfect there, gold and green and deeply meaningful.

In your own temple, sit in the center of your home and radiate golden light throughout as described earlier in this book. You are a sun, a fractal of God Creator.

13

THE SOUND OF HOME

> When we sing we go into a realm of harmony with life—singing from our hearts of joy rather than pain of separation. Then all life sings with us. Life smooths out, flowing with greater ease. — *When I was a Child: as given by the Cosmic Christ*, by Joy-An Tucker

When I was beginning to explore spirituality, I read all of the Medicine Woman series by Lynn Andrews. In her book *Jaguar Woman* one particular statement stood out like a neon sign. Her teacher Zoila explained, "Every form has a sound….Words, sounds, tones, they are all part of what holds reality together. Never is there a life form without sound." I did not know what to do with that knowledge at the time, but the words kept resounding like a gong.

Later on in my spiritual journey, I read *Ascension Handbook* by Tony Stubbs, who explained that every human is a standing vibration. A standing vibration is a combination of all vibratory patterns of emotions and thoughts of a person, which creates an overall frequency. Wow! I was a standing vibration. My standing vibration at that time probably had a lot of anger and confusion in it. We start where we are.

I put that knowledge too in a cubbyhole for safekeeping until I was attracted to a sound healing workshop by Tom Kenyon, a researcher and master of sound healing who worked with an extraterrestrial group of

Hathors, specialists in the use of sound frequencies. I learned that sounds can heal, frequencies can heal.

The first time I used sound for healing was on Eagle, an elegant, spirited chestnut thoroughbred. He had a painful swelling on his pastern joint above his right front foot. I tried poultices for about a month. Then the veterinarian told me invasive surgery was required. My pocketbook said no, and my intuition said, "Why not try healing with sound?"

I set an intention and asked the Hathors to help me make the right sound to heal Eagle's ganglion. Then I bent down close to his lower leg and surrendered. What came out was a series of barks like a seal. Embarrassed, I looked around. Thankfully, there were no other horse owners close by at the boarding stable. I kept making these sounds for a while then stopped. Nothing had changed. The next day, however, the pain and swelling were gone and never returned for the rest of his life. That experience gave me some first hand faith in the power of sound.

I loved dancing to rock and roll music until a book by sound researcher Steve Halpern in those days mentioned that Rock and Roll rhythms were not coherent with healthy body function and explained why. O.k., I didn't stop listening or dancing to rock and roll, but I began to pay attention to how it made me feel. I can only imagine what he might say about heavy metal, which turns the crystals in water—including the water in our own bodies—into an unrecognizable mush. Eventually I began to be more attracted to other kinds of music.

Now it has become common knowledge that sound frequencies can heal the body and influence our emotions for better or worse. The movie, television, and advertising industries use this knowledge for emotional manipulation in every production. More positively, You Tube is full of music based on Solfeggio frequencies (measured in Hertz, Hz) for many kinds of physical and emotional healing and for attuning people to specific vibrations, such as love or peace.

When you bring the sound of music into your inner and outer temple, consider what sounds, lyrics , rhythms, and frequencies feel compatible with love, peace, harmony, joy, balance, and unity. There is music available to encourage any feeling state. You might want to stream baroque classical music, meditation music, solfeggio frequencies, or fun positive lyrics and rhythms into your environment. Experiment, always asking, "How does this sound make me and my body feel?"

Once in the Santa Barbara, California Public Library, a book fell off the shelf in front of me. Its title was *Sacred Harp*. I had been thinking of learning to play an instrument along with feeling doubtful about my musical capabilities. Intrigued, I browsed through it. It was a collection of hymns in four-part harmony for voice only, no instruments. That book was a message to me that I <u>could</u> play an instrument—my voice—a sacred harp. It was a message to me to find my voice and to sing from my heart. Your voice too is a sacred harp.

I started singing in the shower whatever sounds and tones wanted to come forth. The minute water splashed on me, I could not help but sing. Sometimes I asked ascended master Mother Mary to sing through me and just surrendered my voice. Later I dared do that with family or friends. Sometimes I used my sacred harp in a healing or counseling session and encouraged my clients to do the same. So often, simple tones and sounds can express what words cannot. St. Germain has said that when we sing from our hearts, no matter the sound, it is glorious to all creation.

Over time I received more pieces to the puzzle of sound and vibration. Spirit often works in this way. We read something here, hear something there. Then we integrate what we have learned into our own experience. Integration—living the knowledge, owning it—is vital. These pieces can become a whole body of knowledge, a way of life, even a destiny.

Another piece of the puzzle for me was a period of Buddhist focus. During that time I learned by heart thirty-three Sanskrit mantras. (Sanskrit is a very ancient language.) These Sanskrit mantras called in the energetic presence of Buddha and other ascended or enlightened beings. Sometimes they had a specific purpose, such as healing, dispelling harmful energies, helping people transition, blessing humans and animals, quieting the mind, or declarations of intention.

To integrate this understanding, try chanting the words "Quan Yin". Master St. Germain has said that these words, the name of a master of compassion, are a vibrational bridge that creates a geometry that supports the opening of the heart. Whew! That's a lot to grok. That bridge opens to the consciousness of Divine Mother. When you chant "Quan Yin", Divine Mother exists in your heart in that moment. Repeat it for a while. Note how it feels.

Less known powerful mantras are the Essene chants that Yeshua would have used in the spiritual community that he grew up with. You can find "A Mystical Lords Prayer" chanted in Aramaic on You Tube. It seems to have a power that translated versions do not.

For another example, Ascended Master Sananda (Jesus) once gave a three hour transmission through a channel named Eterna on the power of OM, the seed syllable of creation, the first word. When we have envisioned what we want to create, we can use this sound to send it out into all creation to be supported and reflected back to us. I put that lesson into practice by fervently envisioning in detail the place I wanted to live in with my horses. I intended a decent three-bedroom house, ten or more acres set up with corrals for horses, a barn, irrigated green pastures, and a creek running through. I OM'd with all my heart to seal and send my creation.

Manifestation is not always instant although on multi-dimensional New Earth it can be. Ten years later, when I was ready and living in a new place—Mt. Shasta—I was able to manifest everything I asked for and more, including farm equipment, tools, electricity to every corral, a year's worth of hay (all part of the sale) and three paying horse boarders already on the premises. Thank you, Mother Father God! And thank you my beloved Mom and Dad for the inheritance that enabled me to pay for it in full.

Groups in my Temple of New Earth have discussed how they would create New Earth in their own homes. Then we would seal the creation with a group OM from each individual heart. You can OM in this way by yourself or with others for anything you want to create from your heart of love. People have been toning OM for thousands of years. Now you know the creative power of that sound.

RECIPE FOR MANIFESTATION

- BE in the highest vibrational feeling state that you can: love, joy, peace, or just gratitude for what you already have

- IMAGINE in this now moment what you want to create as if it already existed.

- COMMAND your vision into manifestation with the power of your I AM
- OM it into being with love and power.
- RECEIVE the manifestation in this now moment.
- FEEL your joy and gratitude now.
- CELEBRATE!

14

A SPACE OF LOVE

> "I Archangel Michael, invite you, if you can, in your home or wherever, even if it is in your mind, to create a space of love, a space where you can sit or be, that you know emanates love. Let this space remind you to love yourself, to draw upon the love of the universe…to draw upon the love of the Creator, filling yourself with love and taking time each day to recognize that you are bathing in love, and that love is your power." Archangel Michael via Natalie Glasson, Omna.org: *Heart Chakra Implodes and Explodes*

As I sat at my desk in my office, I gazed out the window at the cattle in the field across the street. I noticed the wires on the fences and, a bit closer, the web fences around my own front pasture. Then it occurred to me to notice the space between the wires of these fences. Big deal, right? But this time a knowing flooded me—all space is filled with Source Love, God's love. I didn't just think it. I felt it. I knew it without doubt.

I began looking at all the space around me—between trees, between my computer and modem, between desk and chair. Everywhere I looked I focused on the spaces between things. I felt, almost saw, the frequencies of love, joy, and peace. Considering further the space between electrons, atoms, and cells in my body and in every object around me, I realized how much I and all things are filled with the love of Source. I realized it is a matter of perspective, of attention, of bringing our focus to space which creates the experience. We notice grass in a field but not the air above it unless a strong wind insists. Usually I focus on objects not the space between, and I rarely think of all the space in my body. Even if we humans don't always experience Divine love in spaces, it is worthwhile sometimes to focus on the space between things and notice what happens—an expansion, an opening perhaps.

When creating your own sanctuary of New Earth, consider space and spaciousness. If you have a beautiful piece of art or a flower, let it stand out with space around it so it can be noticed, truly seen and appreciated. Clutter, too many beautiful things, will blunt its impact, just as one fine rose will be lost in the crowd when placed in a bouquet of a dozen roses. The same goes for furniture. Less is more. Create space. Let the space itself vibrate with live plant energy, sunlight, and Source light and love.

There are also the frequencies with which you yourself fill the space. Sit in a room and fill it with gold light or one of the other rays. Call angels to be present if you choose. Some will literally take up residence in your home if you ask. Call in whatever energies resonate with you of the nature kingdoms and light realms. And know that in all that space softly, gently, tenderly radiates love from Source, enfolding, embracing, filling you up.

Filling you up—make space for that. Imagine that all the particles in your body are a little further apart to the degree that feels comfortable to you. That space is already filled with love and light, yet now consciously notice it and let more in. Notice how your inner spaciousness feels. Savor it.

PART 3

UNITY IN RELATIONSHIP

15

CEASE ARGUING! HARMONY IN RELATIONSHIP

I remember watching a movie called *Overcomer*, directed and written by Alex Kendrick, about a high school sports coach whose football program was about to be dropped from the curriculum. He might even lose his job. He was taking out his woundedness, anger, frustration, and depression on his family, especially his wife.

After some biting words to her, he retreated into a full male pout, refusing to look at her. Rather than arguing or biting back, his wife sat on a chair some distance away. Gradually she inched the chair closer to him until she was sitting in front of him. After a few minutes, she spoke to him from her heart, letting him know that for her he was more than just his professional identity. I don't remember her exact words of love and wisdom, only that she broke through until they were able to embrace and he was able to cry.

Another movie that impressed me was *I Prefer Heaven* about the life of Philip Niri, a Catholic priest who was later declared a saint. In that film, a furious young man attacked Philip for interfering with his harmful intentions toward a young boy. Philip was on the ground with the raging man's sword at his throat. In that moment, Philip asked, "Why are you so angry?" His assailant was disarmed by the question and the care behind it.

A few words that describe qualities allowing response instead of reaction are forbearance, divine neutrality, unflappability, and don't forget humor. Asking a question can spin someone from extreme emotion into mind thought. All these qualities combined with compassion can halt the momentum of argument, anger and even aggression.

In my 20's I was in a crazy-in-love (or lust?) relationship that was mutual. But we communicated almost solely through argument for seven years. For some people it can be an intellectual game, the competition of debate. For most it is a desire to impose their beliefs and perspectives on others, a desire to be right, to win. Arguments are often tinged with judgment and complaint, as well. I tolerated seven years of such disharmony, not conscious enough then to realize change was needed or even possible.

The masters of light and St. Germain in particular have told us to cease arguing. CEASE ARGUING! Why is it so important not to be entrapped in argument? We can't go into higher frequencies until we stop fighting one another. St. Germain has said, "Ask the other, how may I serve your heart, and in that we will find a solution together." He continued, "For the solution is already there. You are wired for solution. You bear the frequency of solution, which is love." (from a channeling through Ashamarae McNamara)

Harmony in our homes and on the planet requires a sacrifice of the need to be right. When someone is upset, they are actually hungry for love. Relationship flourishes when we ask within, "How may I serve the other to feel loved?" In St. Germain's words, "It is an honor to serve. It is a gift to serve. It is grace to serve." He cautions us not to go down in frequency to relate. Instead "move through the world in your higher frequencies. Be the great wave. Be your divinity. Vibrate that energy of light, of love, of supreme heart."

In your home temple of New Earth, you can exercise some of the wisdom in this chapter. If other members of your household are not in alignment with your creation of a harmonious temple, however, you must find a way to do it anyway though decoration that has meaning to you or by letting other household members simply co-create harmony with you rather than giving it a label. Ask your family members if they would like more love, joy, peace, harmony, and unity in the home; and ask them for suggestions about how that might be accomplished both inner and outer. Then it becomes a commUNITY project. You can also exemplify the qualities of forbearance and compassion, and shine your light throughout your space of love whether others align with your project or not. If necessary at first, you can focus your love, joy, and intention on just one room. And cease arguing about anything.

Similar to argument, control in relationship is another rock to stumble on. (Just a few days ago, I tripped on a rock and fell flat on my face. A perfect metaphor!) Until I began my New Earth project, my in-home relationships at Joy Rising Ranch were with short and long-term renters. The need to control can damage relationships of any kind.

When I first started renting a room in my home, I wanted to control everything, including the way dishes were placed in the dishwasher. I liked to place smaller dishes and cups in the top rack, which has less vertical room, and the larger dishes in the bottom rack, which had more. I also liked to place dishes as efficiently as possible in the slots to make the best possible use of the space. Almost every renter put the dishes in the dishwasher helter skelter with no consideration of intelligent use of the space and design. When I instructed my often brilliant, creative, non-conformist housemates on how to do it properly, I just created alienation along with non-compliance. I was being too much like a parent.

Eventually I stopped saying anything and rearranged dishes or just let them be. It wasn't worth creating friction to insist on my way. No longer triggered, I even began to chuckle when I saw dishes cattywhompus. And I appreciated my father all the more. He had simply taken over the job of carefully loading the dishwasher every night because my mother's way made no sense at all.

Some of my requirements were no smoking, drugs, or alcohol because I preferred not to live with the low vibes, leaky auras, and dark entity attachments that often accompany such habits. When I made those rules clear to prospective renters, they were usually self-selective. Then Bryan came along.

Bryan reserved my master bedroom two months prior to his arrival and paid for those two months so I would hold the space, which I greatly appreciated. Besides, the picture he sent me had a lot of charisma. He knew my requirements, had a charming Tennessee accent, and was downright forty-eight-years-old-bald headed cute. Although my renters were usually women or couples, he looked to be a comfortable person to have in the house—and he was.

Bryan had sold his house and his business in Tennessee because Archangel Michael had asked him to come to Mt. Shasta to channel Adama, the high priest of Telos. Bryan was to write books about Telos, the fifth-dimensional city associated with Mt. Shasta. He planned to stay with me for six weeks while he looked for a place of his own to make a home for his twin flame, whom he had not yet found.

After he arrived here, he asked me for a bottle for spitting chewing tobacco! I hid my shock and gave him a juice bottle. He also enjoyed craft beer and often colorful language. He was so charming and soulful, so interesting and fun to talk to, his accent so delightful that all my rules dissolved. They had no value or meaning when faced with such a genuine, authentic, life-enjoying man. Oh, and he swept his crumbs off the kitchen counter onto the floor because he thought they would be easier to sweep up. When I thought about it, I decided he might just have a point.

By night Bryan worked with Archangel Michael and his blue ray angels helping clear and clean destructive forces in the world and assisting their victims, a heartrending task. By day he went up the mountain to meet with Adama in consciousness, asking questions and taking notes like a true anthropologist. His daily accounts delighted me, as I became a friend and even a confidant about his love life and search for his twin. After six weeks I was sorry to see him move into his own place, but we remained friends, and I became an editor of his fascinating book, *Telos: Welcoming New Earth* by Bryan Tilghman.

I am so glad I dropped my controls in his case and chose heart opening flexibility instead. Every step we humans take to move out of our old survival patterns brings a new level of freedom, a key to New Earth. By the way, he did find the woman of his dreams—a spirited, playful woman close to Archangel Michael and closer to his own age than the sexy young goddess he had originally imagined.

Intend to bring more harmony into your life, home, relationships, and world both inwardly and outwardly in thought, feeling, and action, no matter the circumstances. It helps to connect to your heart first, to your I AM Presence, or the Flower of Life too. If there is disharmony around you, pause and reset to harmony before taking action. It will get easier with practice.

16

YOUR JOY IS YOUR PASSION

A vital part of relationship to your self and others is living your truth. Sometimes to be practical we live our untruth first rather than live our passion and our joy—and even that may change.

When I was a college English teacher in southern California some years ago, a drought desiccated much of the United States. Crying all summer for rain, the Midwest lost livestock as well as corn. Southern California had received even less than its usual scanty allotment of rainfall that year, and drought conditions had already begun by April. Bear and coyote were migrating down out of the hills, nearing and even entering populated areas. Throughout this region and much of the Southwest, people drew quietly into their own inner circles of trusted friends and danced or prayed for rain.

A woman of the Laguna tribe of dry New Mexico had once taught me that the magic of the rain dance requires becoming in harmony, at-one-ment with oneself, with members of one's family and community, with the surrounding environment, and with spirits of the area. One seeks to be the center point in the crossing of material and spiritual worlds, represented in many cultures by a cross. The rain dance also derives from the belief in the power of directed collective human consciousness. Humans create through thoughts, words, images. What we think, we bring into reality—for better of worse.

In keeping with this understanding, I decided to ask one of my English classes to write freely, welcoming the rain on a late April day with only a few gray clouds in the sky. According to weather forecasts, there was little chance of rain.

After explaining Laguna perspectives to my class, I suggested that as much as we needed the rain, we collectively chase it away with our thoughts. We might say, "I know we need the rain, but not today because I am planning to go biking, or to an outdoor wedding, or to a picnic, or to a horseshow, or to Los Angeles." I proposed that instead we welcome the rain together.

Nature is a mirror for us, I explained. When drought occurs, people heed the environment once again, make the necessary adjustments. In myths and stories drought and wasteland are symbols of aridity of spirit, when people are not living in accordance with divine order. As in the myths we need to realign ourselves with spirit once again, rather than live only to fulfill the needs of our own egos. Allowing the rain to fall means allowing ourselves to be filled with the life-giving waters of spirit, to allow the forces of nature and divinity to work though us.

As they wrote, so did I, resulting in a song asking Thunderbird to touch gently the corn, water the deer. Before the class period was over, a rush of wind whooshed through the Eucalyptus trees outside the classroom window; and even with the sun still shining, rain began to fall.

That creative, magical class was a rare one, however. Most of the time I had to stick to a specific curriculum designed to train students to write research papers, a skill most of my students did not value. When I first started teaching community college, I was full of enthusiasm and creativity, but that got dampened by staff disapproval of my new-age inclinations, my sometimes unconventional teaching style, and book choices that that weren't always classical British or American literature.

Even the approved literary choices were later reduced to collections of short essay samples that seemed boring and depressing to me and to students who didn't really care about the difference between a narrative essay and a comparison/contrast essay or between a comma and a period. At some point I realized I didn't either. I began ordering two books for my students each quarter—the one that was required and the one that taught mastery skills for students and the difference between victim and creator. It inspired many students. Sometimes I would sneak in readings from a captivating piece of literature, such as Child of the Dawn, by Gautama Chopra, who wrote the book when he himself was an undergraduate.

To keep my job, I kept toeing the line (and testing it), slogging along to make the money I needed to take care of myself and my horses. I had bought a young filly soon after earning my first master's degree. Then I bought an older horse to keep her company and to ride while she grew up. They were my passion and my joy, along with her two babies further down the line. Eventually, after 17 years of teaching, I was not rehired. Although the job loss created some chaos and consternation, it was actually a blessing in disguise as it forced me to move on and to reinvent my life. Taking early retirement helped with finances a teensy bit.

St. Germain once said while teaching about the blue indigo ray, which has a bit more purple in it, "Your joy is your passion and your passion is your joy." (St. Germain through Ashamarae McNamara) That rang so true to me, especially since I had lived the opposite in part of my work life. Just as joy is an indigo blue ray quality, so is passion. It is literally our divine blueprint to live our passion and our joy, and so it is on New Earth. We can begin practicing now to create that reality for all. It is my passion and my joy to relate to my horses. It is my passion and joy to fill my home with higher vibrations and décor that reflects them. Even more, however, it is my passion and my joy to share the experience with others, to hold the vision, to co-create New Earth.

1. What is alive in you? What are you passionate about? Whatever it is, be assured that everything is spiritual. Everything.
2. Call forth that feeling of passion into your body.
3. Invoke, if you choose, an indigo blue ray master such as Mother Mary, Yeshua, or Krishna or unnamed, to magnify the energy of passion
4. Tell all of your cells to radiate the indigo blue ray, every cell radiant with sparkling indigo blue.
5. With your inner vision, see or imagine your body filling with blue light.

6. See your aura filling with blue light.
7. Breathe it all in and anchor it into the earth through the base of your spine and the bottoms of your feet.
8. Wiggle your fingers and toes and chuckle at the image of your blueness.

"With passion comes energy, knowing, new tools. Surrendering to new understanding and information, to 'I don't know,' allows the body to open, the cells to open; and your DNA releases the new from its blueprint. What you are passionate about is already recorded in your DNA. You came in with it, programmed for this moment for new passion" (St. Germain through Ashamarae McNamara)

Bring your core passion and joy into relationship with all things, all activities. You bring New Earth to life, here and now.

17

REVERENCE FOR ALL LIFE

> Just being a friend, Beloved Child of God—that is right relationship with your self, other humans, and all creatures who share the planet with you. You have dominion to demonstrate kindness, compassion, love, not to harm, enslave or brutalize. You lead the way to enlightenment and teach by example. —The Cosmic Christ. From *When I was a Child: As Given by the Cosmic Christ* by Joy-An Tucker

One night in a dream, my horse Happy ran into me at a full gallop, then I woke up. I dreamed the same dream three nights in a row. I thought the dream might be warning me to be vigilant and careful around the horses free in pasture to avoid injury. I recited the dream to Ascended Master St. Germain during my next channeled session, which were actually few and far between over the years.

"Where did you feel the impact when he first hit you?" St Germain asked.

"I felt it in my chest," I answered, placing my hand on my heart center.

"Where did he go after that?"

"I don't know," I said as I threw my hands up in the air. "I woke up."

"Exactly," said St Germain. "Your body knows. He jumped over you as your arms just showed. He hit you only with his energy to knock down a heart wall." (A heart wall is an energy shield humans put up to protect themselves emotionally.) "He is a healer and he knew what he was doing. If he had not met your dream body with his in this way, you would have had a heart attack in eighteen weeks,"

I was stunned. I did not know what to say. My horse a shaman healer? No wonder he acted frustrated, angry, or stubborn when I tried to train him for riding in a kind but traditional way. I had imposed my own agenda on him, but he was here for a different purpose.

St Germain went on to explain that Happy also worked with others in dreaming and that he would like to be available as a healer in the physical realm too if I would like to facilitate that.

Happy was born at a boarding stable the year before I bought my property, Joy Rising Ranch. I had rescued his mother at another stable the day before she was to be euthanized because she had equine protozoal myelitis, a kind of horse polio. I had felt her reaching out to me. She knew what was in store for her, and she wanted to live. I told the owner I would like to try to heal her even though the vet said she was not curable. I thought maybe essential oils and energy healing might help.

After I took her under my wing, I researched medicines for the disease and found one alternative from Heartland Vet Supply in the Midwest that combined colloidal silver and ashwaganda root. I also consulted Ascended Master Sananda who told me to change her name, which was Sable, meaning black. Her aura is black, he told me. You must give her a name of light to give her a chance at recovering.

I named her Honey, golden Honey, so every time I said her name she received the projection of honey gold light. It was so easy and natural to call her that. At age four then, Honey was a big, gentle mare, half Percheron, a draft breed. Her former owner had rescued her from a farm that raised horses for meat (often called venison in dog food.) Her disease had caused atrophy in her right hip and right hind leg. Her muscles on that side were like jello, and her right hind leg was thinner and shorter than the other.

After three months of treatment and full time pasture, Honey's right hip became stronger but slanted, and the leg was still short.

"You have done as much as you can with the medication," said Sananda. "The protozoa in her are greatly reduced, so her immune system can keep the balance as long as you never use any kind of drug on her."

"No vaccines or anything?" I asked

"No. No drugs. They would throw her immune system off balance." He added, "She wants a foal"

I was flabbergasted. "No way!" I already have three horses that I can't afford, and bringing up another baby is not on my agenda."

"It's your free choice, as always." Sananda replied.

"Can she have a baby safely," I asked, already feeling myself softening. "It would be hard on her wouldn't it?"

"She can handle it."

My resistance to the idea melted after a few days. After I spent a few months looking for a sire—a smaller horse so the baby would wind up smaller than Honey—the deed was done. Happy was born eleven months later.

After St Germain had encouraged me to start a healing with horses program with grown-up Happy, he became Doc Happy. Doc Happy could not always tell if a visitor was a client or just there for a more superficial connection. He asked for a sign. I agreed to send him a telepathic image of a cartoon horse with big black-rimmed glasses and a stethoscope. He liked that.

After I had been doing healing sessions with grown-up Happy for about a year, it was clear that Honey wanted to participate and was already doing so from the other side of the fence. I stopped separating them during the sessions. They became an awesome healing team, sometimes working on the client together, sometimes taking turns according to what they deemed was needed. I too am a healing guide during the sessions, preparing the clients with a meditation to quiet their minds and open their hearts before entering the corral—the doctor's office.

All animals, not just horses and domestic pets, have talents, understanding, and wisdom that humans rarely notice or acknowledge. They are our partners on this planet. On New Earth so it is. We can start preparing and practicing right now. We can create the reality of reverence for all life right now, and so it shall be.

18

ONENESS WITH ALL LIFE

Reverence for all life begets oneness with all life and vice versa. One day I walked up the country road that runs in front of my home. Across the street is a cow pasture. Farther up it becomes wooded with a creek gurgling merrily beside the road. That day as I reached the wooded area, I suddenly felt and saw the trees differently, perhaps because my mind was peaceful enough to let truth in. I felt, not just thought, that the trees were all expressions of Source, just as I am. Pure love surrounded me on both sides of the road. Every tree and bush was God, Creator, who dwells in all of her creation, bar none. My heart expanded ecstatically with love in return. This was more than an intellectual understanding, and I was so grateful for this gift.

Try an intentional shift in perspective yourself with just one tree. With a soft gaze, intend to see it as an expression of Creator. Then note if that makes any difference in your perception or the feeling in your body. If nothing happens, that's ok. A seed has been planted that will grow into a tree of many branches, leaves, and colorful blossoms. The seed knows nothing yet of the impact it will have on other beings just by standing there and being itself.

Every part of creation is part of the whole, the One, uniquely experiencing and expressing. There is no separation from the One except from the unconscious level of the personality self, or ego. How can we not love and embrace the Divine in all things, in every atom and electron of creation? A personality may misqualify the God energy in service to self, but at their core one and all will eventually awake to their unity. How can any being that knows every creation equally houses God, Source, Creator ever harm another one of itself?

On the New Earth this knowing and understanding is a given, the reality. That is why no being harms another. Harmfulness simply does not exist—only love, wisdom, trust, innocence, which at its roots means "not to harm".

Make this innocence your own reality as you create your inner and outer temple of New Earth. As has been said, become as a child to enter the kingdom of heaven. (Bible, many versions)

19

KIND EYES

I saw the phrase somewhere—kind eyes. It might have been in the subject line of an unread, unsolicited email I deleted, but the words reverberated in my mind. I paid attention. I experimented. With intention I looked at my surroundings with kind eyes. Yes. That felt different from my usual way of seeing. It created a good feeling, especially in my heart. My eyes felt more soft and relaxed. I felt more connected to everything I gazed upon. I felt like a loving mother looking at her baby.

Try it yourself. Does it change the way you feel? Does it change your perspective?

The next time I went out to the horses, I looked at them with kind eyes. For a few months I had been relating to them as an overburdened caretaker, just getting the job done—horses fed, horsed turned out, corrals cleaned, horses brought in, lawn mowed, fields irrigated, cats fed, house cleaned and so on. I had been working without passion, feeling the grind. All of the horses liked having their bellies scratched because flies congregate there and leave itchy bites. Honey especially appreciated the service. Feeling loving kindness every time I had any interaction with her, I scratched her belly from behind her front legs all the way back to her udder. She showed her pleasure by lifting her spine a bit and stretching out her head and neck. I enjoyed it also because she would reach around and groom me too with her strong lips. It made me laugh when she found my bare skin under my shirt. Often she aimed for my lower back when I had pain there. Every time she massaged me there, the pain disappeared. She was returning kindness with kindness.

Several months after I started this routine, during a session with St. Germain, he said to me out of the blue, unrelated to other discussion: "Your mare had a cancer tumor on her udder. Your kind touch healed her. You have learned the frequency of kindness."

In your own home and life, you can practice kindness if you choose. Look with kind eyes at people and surroundings. Let that expand into acts of kindness. Loving kindness is a frequency worth nurturing. It can revitalize your life and relationships, and it just plain feels good.

20

FREEDOM

Ah! Freedom! Run, leap, buck with joy within yourselves, Beloveds. You are set free of the pen of your limited perspectives and beliefs. The gate is open. Dash through! From *When I Was a Child: As given by the Cosmic Christ*, by Joy-An Tucker

When I turn my horses out to pasture every morning, how joyful they are to be free, running, rearing, bucking, inspiring each other's play. Even though they have large paddocks, it isn't the same as the greater freedom of spacious pastures. I wish I could leave them out all day and all night, but the grass is too rich, too high in sugar. If the horses eat too much, their feet may become inflamed, leading to excruciating painful destruction of the feet and ultimate death of the horse. Therefore I bring them in after only four hours of early morning grazing when the sugar is lower.

When I go to round them up, I use intention and body language, not a whip, to move them toward the corrals. I point and say, "Go on in!" I also have a food reward waiting, but I usually don't give them a choice. It's for their own good.

A horse in freedom would likely graze twenty hours a day, so they are reluctant to leave their delicious green grass. I twirl a lead rope a bit and raise my energy a notch, point and say more strongly, "Go on in!" One begins to move, and the rest soon follow. That is their choice.

Doc Happy will go with the herd until he is near the corrals, then he hangs back and continues to graze. I tell him he can stay out just a bit longer until the other horses are in their respective places, then I come back for him. He keeps eating. I know from experience that if I try to halter him to lead him, he will pull away with great strength and determination; so I do not halter him. Do I get angry and smack his butt with a whip or let him have choice?

I do not like to treat animals as slaves. Creator gave humans freedom of choice to have our experiences; humans usually do not extend that choice to animals or even to other humans or themselves.

Happy waits to see what I will do and keeps eating. He does not fear me, thank God. God is pure love and never to be feared. How can I be like God?

When horses want to move each other, they will nip each other on the butt, no hard feelings. So I strengthen my intent, shake my rope at his behind, point to his corral, and say more loudly—but without anger or aggression—"Happy! Go on in!!" No compliance. I give him a tap on his rear end with the rope. I think he is laughing at me. He is deliberately testing my will. It's as if he is saying, "Recognize that I too am sovereign."

In the past I sometimes lost my temper, but that destroys bonding and relationship, creating mistrust not respect. I choose to stay in loving neutrality instead. Within that calm I bite him on the butt with the rope a little harder. He doesn't blink an eye and keeps eating.

"OK HAPPY! I really need you to go in so your feet stay healthy!" Whap!

"Oh, do you really mean it? Ok. No big deal." He saunters away from the grass into the corral as I walk companionably beside him with an arm over his back and give him a piece of carrot when the gate closes behind him.

"Thank you, kind sir," I say. "I love you so much!"

In this way, Happy has asserted his self-authority for a moment to make me recognize he is a sovereign being with a mind and feelings of his own, at the same time requiring me to assert my will—which was weak most of my life—with love and humor. It is a game. Often now I honor his choice by letting him graze a little longer (but I start bringing them all in sooner). Then he is ready by his own choice to come in. I believe it is a conscious and purposeful lesson on his part. He is a good teacher.

We humans must give up needing to control everything to feel secure.

That is a survival mechanism born of fear. That behavior pattern has served a purpose, and now we are evolving beyond it. For example, during one healing session with both Doc Happy and Honey, a man from India who worked in a Silicon Valley technology industry stood between Happy and Honey. They had already been working with him energetically for a while. Suddenly both horses turned away from him at the same time, leaving him standing alone. Watching from outside the corral, I wanted to run in and guide them back. I was afraid he would feel abandoned (which would be something to work on) or think that the session was not worth it, But I talked myself down and decided to trust and allow instead of trying to control the situation.

The man stood there for a few minutes, then walked over to each horse, stroking and thanking them. Now was the time to go in with some carrots. I asked him how the session had felt to him.

"When the horses turned away from me, I was suddenly flooded with white light. I experienced that only once before in a ceremony when I was a child in India."

Thank God I trusted the horses and myself and did not interfere with his experience. Happy and Honey knew exactly what they were doing.

On New Earth no one dominates another. No one takes another's freedom of choice, and no one harms another. Horses run free and interact with humans in wise friendship, as do other animals. Since all are consciously God beings, and since God is pure comprehensive love, fear is unknown.

For a practical example of allowing choice on pre-New Earth, it is important to give choice to children and frail adults. "It's time for bed now." (not arguable). "Do you want us to read you this book or that?" or "You can't stay safely in your home by yourself any longer. (not arguable). Do you choose to live here or there?" or "Do you choose this caretaker or that?" Or you might just let the other make his/her own choice and experience the consequences, as Creator does. Let us begin now to create heaven on earth by letting go of the need to control, seeing with God's eyes and heart, never judging, allowing freedom of choice as long as no harm is done and is in the highest good of all concerned.

Question to ask yourself for self-awareness:
- How and when do I try to control others?

- How do I limit my own choices?
- How do I limit choices of others?
- How might I do things more in alignment with Freedom?

21

FREEDOM OF THE UNKNOWN

Another kind of freedom is the freedom of not knowing, a part of passion and joy. When you decorate your house, for example, you can choose to have no plan, no map other than your intention to change or create. Begin by having a sense of the feeling vibrations, the qualities you want to have in your home. From that feeling state—let us say love or peace or harmony—let it flow from there. Ideas and visions will come to you or something will pop out at you on a store shelf or showroom or on the internet because that is what you are attracting. Allow discovery and surprise as so often happened to me. When I saw a green and gold papasan chair online, it was accidental. I was looking for something else—a more traditional cushy chair. The papasan was perfect—round, lightweight, leggy, and easily moved.

Not knowing is highly underrated. When we let go of the need to control, to know every little step ahead of time and instead step into the unknown, into not knowing, big and little miracles and synchronicities can happen. Oddly it is through not knowing that true inner knowing can happen beyond mental concepts. Again we surrender to Creator, the God presence within. Most people have heard the phrase "let go and let God." Another might say, "Beloved I AM, take command of all that I am. Let me see through your eyes and heart, feel, speak, act through your heart." (from a decree by Asara, teloschannel.com)

It is ok not to know in your mind what is your next step. You might even make a practice of it to learn to trust your intuition. You can ask Creator to guide you. Ask Creator in your own heart, "What is my next step?" instead of arranging everything from your mind based on what you already know. For example, a woman who came to work with Doc Happy and Honey told me that she recently felt she must leave her job and home. When she asked her inner guidance where she should go, she received the words "North Carolina". Her mother thought she was crazy or beyond foolish. I supported her choice and advised her to keep following her inner guidance on her journey east. She felt excited about the adventure into the unknown. She had wanted one more visit with the horses before leaving.

Answers to your questions will come in many ways—direct knowing, through another person, a phrase that you read, while weeding your garden, a comment on the internet, the eyes of a dog. Who knows? Ultimately all knowing comes from silence, the stillness within the center of all things, the ocean beneath the surface waves. Let the space between things be a doorway to you know not what. That not knowing is your freedom. Seriously, play with it. Imagine stepping through a space between fence rails or chair legs as if stepping through a door. What do you experience? Maybe nothing, maybe a feeling state, maybe a vision. Or stand before an imaginary beaded curtain. Imagine it is a doorway to the light realms or New Earth. Open the curtain and step through.

We are all about to experience a whole new reality as we become closer in resonance to New Earth. We don't know what it will be like to live in crystalline light bodies beyond duality, never lacking anything, one with other humans and all life, happy. We don't know what new colors we will see or what such high vibrations will feel like. We don't know if the mountain before us now might instead be a valley. We don't know what it will be like to exist side by side with our enlightened galactic brothers and sisters. We don't know what wonderful technologies will assist us. We don't know how it will be to live in a world without conflict. We are stepping through a doorway into we know not what. We are free.

As you create a temple of New Earth in your own home, you are also building a Creator's ashram, a place of connection and staying connected with Creator. So let Creator be your guide. Why not?

22

DOLPHINS AND RAINBOWS

As I walked along a Santa Barbara, California beach one day, I saw a pod of dolphins leaping through the waves offshore, swimming parallel to me. Suddenly a song, both words and music, arose in my mind and heart. The dolphins were singing to me! In one verse they sang of rainbows:

There are rainbows all around you,

Black, red, yellow, white,

And on the other side of raindrops,

They are all one light.

Animals and people, rocks and plants and sky,

A rainbow bridge connects us all

If you believe, you will not fall

As once fell the dolphins,

Singers of the sea.

They continued, "See the rainbow bridge now connecting you and me, you a child of the land, I a dolphin of the sea."

Rainbows are so uplifting when we see them in the sky. Raindrops have become prisms for sunlight, onelight. In this verse the dolphins sing about unity, the norm on New Earth. Rainbows are a reflection of diversity in oneness and the importance of conscious connection. The seven rainbow colors are the seven master rays sent forth from Creator. At some level, a memory deep in our DNA, we feel that rainbow connection and oneness with Creator, a feeling of elation and joy.

To bring the magic of rainbows and all that they inspire into my temple of New Earth, I hung glass prisms in my windows. Rainbows dance in all the rooms when the sun shines through. I remember hippies hanging prisms in their windows in the 1960's too, and humanity has evolved since then even more. Now we know that everything is vibratory energy. Every emotion, hue, and color holds a vibratory frequency. When you are holding vibrations of love, peace, joy, harmony, and unity, you are certain to have rainbows around you. You are ascending for that moment into your rainbow light body.

In your own home, you may be inspired to express rainbows in some way. And whenever you talk to another, see or imagine a rainbow bridge connecting you. Notice how that feels.

Next see or imagine a rainbow bridge now connecting you and God, Creator—however you envision that being. I once asked Ascended Master Sananda to describe him, knowing that every description is a bridge to something indescribable.

He is infinitely wise and all-knowing and like an innocent child at the same time, answered Sananda. He loves to laugh and to hear your joy and laughter.

St. Germain and other ascended masters often refer to the Creator of this universe as the Great Central Sun or the consciousness of the Great Central Sun. Creator is also described as formless and limitless, containing all form, yet is incredibly present and accessible because there is no separation except in human minds. These are also descriptions of you, your I AM God presence, the fractal of God that you are.

I feel most connected to our Creator as described by Sananda. I also often envision Creator as Divine Mother in the form of Mother Mary or Quan Yin. Whatever works for you will create the bridge of connection and heart-to-heart communication with Creator if that is your intention. And remember you are not actually separate. You can talk to God in your own heart.

Shortly after I wrote this chapter, I went to a friend's moving sale. There on a wall hung a round stained glass depiction of two dolphins leaping up, forming two arcs like a heart, touching their noses together. Of course, I bought it and hung it in my gold room. It added playful vitality to the room.

23

CONNECTING WITH CREATOR

Om Sat Om Na Om Na

This Sanskrit chant is a sound vibration that creates the most beautiful alignment with all that is Creator and serves your connection with Creator. *Om* is the vibrational form of Creator. *Sat* is the Divine foundation of reality itself. (Archangel Metatron through Natalie Glasson at omna.org). I like to chant it, sing it, dance it, have fun with it, play with it. Creator loves to laugh, and dance and play with us. Our joy is his. *OmNa* is the bliss and ecstasy that can be experienced through connection with Creator. Our bliss is hers.

Another way I like to connect with Creator is with a glass of water that I keep beside my bed. Holding the glass in front of me, I say, "Great Central Sun, please infuse my water." Then I relax and allow. Sometimes immediately and sometimes within a half minute, I feel a charge of energy around me and see feel that energy coming into my water. It expands, gets stronger, a little more intense. "Thank you," I say and take two sips. Then I set it on my night table and hope my cat doesn't find it. When I drink more later, I remember that it is infused by Creator and appreciate more sips. It feels good going down, joining Creator's vibration with the water of my body. I leave a few sips to pour into the cat's water in the morning.

Prayer, of course, is another way to connect or simply have a conversation with that One who is always there with you and within you. Yes. Talk to Creator. Allow yourself to feel an energetic response. For instance, just now as

I sat on my blue sofa with a writing journal in my lap, I said "Creator, what needs to be written right now? What do you want to say to humanity?"

Then I felt Creator's presence throughout my body, so nurturing, peaceful, and loving. That's it! I felt supremely loved. All my cells vibrated deliciously faster. My cat Shanti, a Sanskrit word for peace, jumped into my lap. He felt it too....

There are no words for what I am conveying here. All I can say is STOP. Breathe into your heart. Talk to Creator yourself. Feel the response. Listen for the wisdom, the knowing that comes directly and personally to you.

What do you want to co-create with Creator? Write it down, then speak it out loud. Ask Creator to invent through you, dance through you, sing through you, paint through you, plant tomatoes through you, speak to a child through you—anything you choose. Then receive and allow.

.....I am feeling the love more than ever now. Although at first, I felt it in every cell, it was most vital in my heart center. Now I feel it expanding in my second chakra, the tummy area just below my navel, the creative center of our bodies. A release, a clearing is happening there, a healing! Joy is there, a feeling that all I want to do is create, create, create. Creator is present in me. I AM Creator too. And so are you.

The love in my heart and joy in my belly effortlessly radiate and grow. It is their nature to shine. "Beloved Creator, thank you for creativity. Thank you for enabling me to shine your presence into the world wherever I am, whatever I do. May I be a tuning fork for others. Thank you!"

A glass of water sits near me. I hold it tenderly for a moment with both hands. I softly blow these precious frequencies into it. I drink.

Now I rest and allow the experience to integrate. I feel the comfort of my blue velvet sofa, feel the dynamic beauty of the unicorn rearing on the wall behind me, appreciate the blue sun on the wall across the room. I look with kind eyes at the lush plants by the window. My cat is peaceful in my lap, and White Buffalo Woman framed on my wall to the left is handing forth the long stemmed medicine pipe, so people would learn to talk to Great Spirit. Through the large archway between rooms, I see my newest white orchid, tinged with yellow, rising perkily on its stem in the gold ray room. In my mouth I still taste my breakfast of multi-grain sourdough bread slathered with cashew cream cheese and strawberry jam. My feet on the floor, I anchor

God's gift into Mother Earth. So grateful, so grateful I AM.

I sit in my Temple of New Earth, Creator's Ashram, my home. All is well. May it be so for you.

AFTERWORD

Let us all join together to hold the vision. A basic law of the universe is "What you focus on expands." So let us focus on New Earth, bringing it home right here, right now, in your own home and life. Be it.

I would love to hear if my book has inspired you in any way. Send a note to templeofnewearth@gmail.com   And pass it on.

Many blessings on your own journey,

Joy-An Tucker

www.joyrisingranch.com

ADDITIONAL READING AND LISTENING

BOOKS

Aurelia Louise Jones, *The Seven Sacred Flames*

Bryan Tilghman, *Telos: Welcoming New Earth*

Eckhart Tolle, *New Earth: Awakening to Your Life's Purpose*

J. Allen Boone, *Kinship with All Life*

Joy-An Tucker *When I Was a Child: As Given by the Cosmic Christ*

Peter Mt. Shasta, Apprentice to the Masters: *Adventures of a Western Mystic. Vol. 2*

VIDEO/AUDIO

Asara Adams at teloschannel.com   This site archives an outstanding series of transmissions in 2022 on the seven sacred rays. Subscription required

Natalie Glasson, omna.org   Years of free archives of teachings and messages from angels, ascended masters, galactic families of light, and more. A good way to introduce yourself to all of these realms.

TheStargateExperienceAcademy.com   A Pleiadian personal transformation connection with many free archives of webinars and meditations.

www.ingramcontent.com/pod-product-compliance
Lightning Source LLC
Chambersburg PA
CBHW061203010526
44110CB00064B/2668